CHILDREN OF THE MASSACRE

Studies in Chinese Christianity

G. Wright Doyle and Carol Lee Hamrin,
Series Editors

A Project of the Global China Center

www.globalchinacenter.org

Previously published volumes in the series

Carol Lee Hamrin & Stacey Bieler, eds., *Salt and Light: Lives of Faith That Shaped Modern China*, volume 1

Carol Lee Hamrin & Stacey Bieler, eds., *Salt and Light: More Lives of Faith That Shaped Modern China*, volume 2

Richard R. Cook & David W. Pao, eds., *After Imperialism: Christian Identity in China and the Global Evangelical Movement*

Carol Lee Hamrin & Stacey Bieler, *Salt and Light: More Lives of Faith That Shaped Modern China*, volume 3

Lit-sen Chang, *Wise Man from the East: Lit-sen Chang (Zhang Lisheng)*

George Hunter McNeur, *Liang A-Fa: China's First Preacher, 1789–1855*

Eunice V. Johnson, *Timothy Richard's Vision: Education and Reform in China, 1880–1910*

G. Wright Doyle, *Builders of the Chinese Church: Pioneer Protestant Missionaries and Chinese Church Leaders*

Jack R. Lundbom, *On the Road to Siangyang: Covenant Mission in Mainland China 1890–1949*

Brent Fulton, *China's Urban Christians: A Light That Cannot Be Hidden*

Andrew T. Kaiser, *The Rushing on of the Purposes of God: Christian Missions in Shanxi since 1876*

Li Ma & Jin Li, *Surviving the State, Remaking the Church: A Sociological Portrait of Christians in Mainland China*

Linda Banks and Robert Banks, *Through the Valley of the Shadow: Australian Women in War-Torn China*

Arthur Lin, *The History of Christian Missions in Guangxi, China*

Linda Banks and Robert Banks, *They Shall See His Face: The Story of Amy Oxley Wilkinson and Her Visionary Work among the Blind in China*

Robert Banks and Linda Banks, *Children of the Massacre: The Extraordinary Story of the Stewart Family in Hong Kong and West China*

Children of the Massacre

The Extraordinary Story of the Stewart Family
in Hong Kong and West China

Robert and Linda Banks

PICKWICK *Publications* · Eugene, Oregon

CHILDREN OF THE MASSACRE
The Extraordinary Story of the Stewart Family in Hong Kong and West China

Studies in Chinese Christianity

Copyright © 2021 Robert and Linda Banks. All rights reserved. Except for brief quotations in critical publications or reviews, no part of this book may be reproduced in any manner without prior written permission from the publisher. Write: Permissions, Wipf and Stock Publishers, 199 W. 8th Ave., Suite 3, Eugene, OR 97401.

Pickwick Publications
An Imprint of Wipf and Stock Publishers
199 W. 8th Ave., Suite 3
Eugene, OR 97401

www.wipfandstock.com

PAPERBACK ISBN: 978-1-6667-2503-2
HARDCOVER ISBN: 978-1-6667-2035-8
EBOOK ISBN: 978-1-6667-2036-5

Cataloguing-in-Publication data:

Names: Banks, Robert, author. | Banks, Linda, author.

Title: Children of the massacre : the extraordinary story of the Stewart family in Hong Kong and West China / Robert and Linda Banks.

Description: Eugene, OR : Pickwick Publications, 2021. | Studies in Chinese Christianity | Includes bibliographical references.

Identifiers: ISBN: 978-1-6667-2503-2 (paperback). | ISBN: 978-1-6667-2035-8 (hardcover). | ISBN: 978-1-6667-2036-5 (ebook).

Subjects: LSCH: subject | subject | Hong Kong. | China--History.

Classification: call number 2021 (print). | call number (ebook).

Except in primary sources, Scripture quotations are taken from the Holy Bible, New International Version®, NIV® Copyright © 1973, 1978, 1984, 2011 by Biblica, Inc.® Used by permission. All rights reserved worldwide.

Cover Photo: Stewarts with their children born in China, circa 1885.

To Nelson and Davina Yuen,
whose generous hospitality in Hong Kong
has helped make this book possible

Contents

Sources of Images | ix
List of Images | xi
References to Places | xiii
*Acknowledgment*s | xv
Prologue | xvii

1 An Irish Family in the East (1875–1895) | 1
2 Finding a Place in the World (1895–1905) | 26
3 Unfinished Business in China (1905–1914) | 47
4 Experiences of Loss and Love (1914–1925) | 71
5 Living Through Troubled Times (1925–1938) | 96
6 War Erupts on the Home Front (1939–1945) | 119
7 With an Eye to the Future (1945–1958) | 142
   Epilogue | 165
   Appendix: Australian Connections with the Stewart Family | 167

Bibliography | 169

Sources of Images

THE AUTHORS WISH TO thank the following individuals and organisations for permission to reproduce their material in this book:

Banks Family Collection—03; 07; 08

Duncan Robertson Photos, found via Gwulo.com—33

Hope Family Collection—04

Michael Prettejohn Family Photo Collection, found via Gwulo.com—32

Pooler Family Photos—19; 28

Stewart Family Collection—Cover; 01; 05; 09; 14; 20; 27; 30; 38

Taylor Family Photos—11; 13; 17; 18; 22; 26; 40

Church Missionary Society Archives—6

Donald Robinson Library, Moore Theological College—10

Friends of Islington Museum—31

Great War Photos (Paul Reed)—21

Wikipedia Commons—02

Special Collections, Yale University—15

St Paul's College, Hong Kong—23; 24; 37; 39

St Stephen's College, Hong Kong—29; 36

Wellington College, Berkshire, Archives—16

World War 1 Cemeteries—12

All remaining images—25, 34, 35—are in the public domain.

List of Images

Cover: Stewarts with their children born in China, circa 1885

01 Early Sketches of Robert and Louisa | 3
02 Gortleitragh in Black Rock, Dublin | 11
03 Louisa and Robert with Mrs Ahok | 17
04 Robert with Chinese exhibits in Australia | 19
05 Herbert and Evan before trip | 22
06 Summer Mission houses in Hwasang | 29
07 Graves of massacre victims | 34
08 Commission of Inquiry in Foochow | 35
09 Kathleen and Mildred at Brighton Lodge | 41
10 James (3rd from left, back row) at Moore College | 44
11 Arthur as a Curate in London | 46
12 Victoria Harbour, Hong Kong, early 1900s | 48
13 Mildred before going to China | 52
14 Kathleen with Bishop and Mrs Lander | 55
15 West China University Administration Building | 57
16 Evan (behind Master) at Blucher House | 61
17 James at the Student Hostel, Chengtu | 66
18 Reg going to propose to Mildred | 68
19 Philip in full military dress | 72
20 Evan in early years of the war | 78
21 Soldiers' graves in Bethune Town Cemetery | 80

List of Images

22 Mildred and Lionel with Mrs Song | 83

23 Original site of St Paul's College | 85

24 Three Stewarts (1st row, center) with staff in 1920 | 88

25 Hong Kong in the mid-1920s | 97

26 Mildred and family in England | 99

27 Evan and Dorothy's wedding | 105

28 Philip at St Stephen's College | 111

29 New St Stephen's campus at Stanley | 114

30 Ernest and Kathleen in the late 1930s | 118

31 Air raid damage in Islington during Blitz | 122

32 Group of Volunteer Defence Force, 1940 | 123

33 Ward in Tweed Bay Hospital | 130

34 Inside dormitory at Stanley Internees Camp | 133

35 Kathleen's grave at Stanley Military Cemetery | 141

36 Memorial Window to war victims at SSC | 146

37 Evan and Dorothy at St Paul's Sports Day, 1954 | 151

38 Evan Stewart, DSO, OBE, ED | 153

39 Memorial Service at SPC for Evan | 155

40 James C. Y. Yen in China | 157

41 Bishop and Mrs Song | 159

References to Places

To preserve the historical atmosphere and avoid confusion when reading quotes from primary sources, the older spelling of place names in China has been retained:

Canton (Guangzhou)

Chengtu (Chengdu)

Chungking (Chongqing)

Foochow (Fuzhou)

Formosa (Taiwan)

Fukien (Fujian)

Kucheng (Gutian)

Kuliang (Guling)

Kwantung (Guangzhong)

Mienchow (Mianyang)

Nanking (Nanjing)

Peking (Beijing)

Szechwan (Sichuan)

Swatow (Shantou)

Tientsin (Tianjin)

Tungchwan (Dongchuan)

In addition, imperial rather than metric distance measurements have been used in the main text to correspond with quotations from the time.

Acknowledgments

MORE THAN SIXTY YEARS ago Bishop Ronald Hall of Hong Kong wrote "Someday the full story of the Stewart family must be written." For nearly a decade we have felt challenged by his words, but researching and writing biographies of Australian missionaries to China was our first priority. However, the Stewarts' influence kept surfacing even in these stories, and would not leave us alone. During several trips to China in that period, we were able to access sites and research materials connected to the Stewart family. Finally, in 2020, we gave our full attention to not only locating archival sources but also descendants of the Stewart family around the world who had first-hand memories and materials. In doing this, we found more than we could have ever hoped, enabling us to write the untold, remarkable stories of the six orphaned children of the so-called "Kucheng Massacre."

We are very grateful for the assistance received from the many institutions that have made this book possible, namely the Church Missionary Society Archives, Adam Matthew Digital Collections; and Hong Kong Sheng Kung Hui Archives. Also St Paul's College, Hong Kong, especially the Principal, Dennis Yuen, and Wai Sze Wong; St Stephen's College, Hong Kong, its Principal Carol Yang, and Kwok Pui Chan; the Australian National Australian Library, St Mark's Library, Canberra, and Donald Robinson Library in Moore Theological College Library, Sydney.

In particular, we appreciate the contribution made by various Stewart family members in England, Ireland, and Australia. Michael Stewart, Evan's son, has spent hours gathering and sharing materials, patiently and generously answered numerous emails and connected us to various members of the wider family. His, and other family members, trust in our doing justice to his family's story is a great honor. We are also grateful to Joan Mosley, Arthur's daughter, for her personal insights; David Taylor and family, Mildred's grandchildren, for family memorabilia; and both the Pooler family,

Philip's daughter and grandson, as well as Peter Ride and Sue Gaardboe, Arthur's grandchildren, for some photos and materials.

Others who helped us were George Ngu and Xiaxia Xue (Chinese translation), Geoffrey Emerson (Hong Kong connections), and Peter Cunich (Hong Kong historical sites). Once again, our good friend Andrew Lu has provided us with some financial support, and G. Wright Doyle and Carol Hamrin have welcomed our book into Global China Center's Studies in Chinese Christianity Series.

Robert and Linda Banks
February 2021

Prologue

WALKING UP THE STEEP path through a forest of bamboo, we caught a glimpse of a cleared area recognisable from archival photos. Our Chinese guides were surprised at our interest in two vacant plots of ground on the edge of the small village. It had taken us well over three hours drive by mini-van from Fuzhou to reach this isolated spot high in the mountains. Ascending a terraced area, we could just make out the foundations of a building that had once stood there. A few meters further up, on a second terrace, we finally found what we were looking for. This peaceful, almost ethereal, setting was where the so-called "Kucheng massacre" had happened over a century before. Captivated by this story through our research on mission in China, we felt both humbled and honored to be there, especially knowing that only one foreigner had ever visited this site. Reflecting on the horrific events of 1st August 1895, though it had started raining we couldn't leave until we'd read a Bible passage and sung a hymn the missionaries would have known. Heading back down the hill, we made a commitment to tell the story, not only of those who had died but also of its impact on the children who were left behind.

The authors at Hwasang in 2012

1

An Irish Family in the East
(1875–1895)

ROBERT STEWART, A YOUNG Irish lawyer preparing for entrance to the Bar in London, found himself drawn to an evening service at Holy Trinity Church in Richmond. It was April 1875, and he was curious to find out why this church was attracting a growing number of people. Evan Hopkins, its Vicar, had a reputation as a persuasive preacher, whose approach to the Christian faith was both intellectually and personally challenging. Hopkins's text that night was "Looking unto Jesus. . .who, for the joy set before him endured the Cross, despising the shame . . ." (Hebrews 12:2 KJV). "The words went straight to Robert Stewart's heart. This was a new thought—Jesus contemplating man's redemption with joy . . . setting his teeth and doggedly going through with a difficult task . . . even though for Him it meant a Cross!"[1] At the conclusion of the service, he stayed for an 'after-meeting' where Hopkins urged those present to go beyond their previous spiritual experience, and dedicate themselves fully to Christ. After doing this, Robert went back to his rooms in London and lay awake wondering what this would mean for his future.[2]

Over the following weeks this became clear. Despite expectations of a brilliant career in Law following his Honours degree at Trinity College

---

1. Wittenbach, Foreword, 3.

2. The sermons Hopkins preached around this time were collected in a book entitled *Life and Godliness* that appeared a few years later. He had been influenced by teaching that was at the heart of the Keswick Movement, whose first annual Convention took place in the summer of 1875. On the importance of this movement for missionary work, particularly in China, see further Banks, "Keswick Movement", 49–72.

Dublin, Robert believed God was calling him to become a missionary. After talking this over with his family in Dublin, he shared his decision with a few people he was closest to, including Louisa Smyly, a childhood friend with whom he was developing a special relationship. Louisa was the eldest daughter of a family that moved in the same social circle as the Stewarts. Just twenty-three, two years younger than Robert, she had been educated by governesses and a finishing school in Europe. Attractive, petite, and well-read, Louisa played the piano and spoke fluent French. Her strong faith was expressed through working among destitute children in the Smyly Homes and, Schools, among, whom she was "a great favourite."[3]

With a mixture of excitement and apprehension, Robert applied to the Church Missionary Society (CMS) in London and was accepted. Shortly after, he moved into the CMS Training College in Islington to begin a year's study. There he developed a friendship with another university graduate, Llewelyn Lloyd, who was hoping to serve in China. Alongside studying the Bible, Church History, Comparative Religion, Apologetics, and Mission Geography, students were able to gain mission experience through working among the poor, unemployed, and immigrant groups living around them in the East End of London.

As the months went by Robert also developed an interest in China. In Islington he had opportunity to meet Chinese people and visit their homes. For the first time he saw a Confucian Temple, and was shocked to come across opium-dens on some streets. Among the magazines in the Training Centre's library, he found the first issue of the China Inland Mission (CIM) magazine, which talked about the great need of the country with its vast number of unreached people. (As it happened, Hudson Taylor, the founder of CIM was on furlough in Islington at this time, staying less than a couple of miles away, so it is likely that Robert heard, even met, him). In CMS's own magazine, the *Church Missionary Gleaner*, he came across an article by an Irish Anglican missionary, Rev John Wolfe, head of the Mission in Fukien (now Fujian) province on the need for more workers there. Robert was delighted when word came from the CMS General Secretary that both he and Lloyd had been appointed to Foochow (now Fuzhou), capital of the province.

In March 1876, at the end of his course at Islington, Robert returned to Dublin. During the past twelve months, he and Louisa had regularly exchanged letters, and the first thing he did was arrange a visit to her home in fashionable Merrion Square. Ushered into the parlour by the servants, he was greeted by Louisa and her widowed mother. Following a brief

---

3. Watson, *In Life and Death*, 157.

conversation over afternoon tea, he and Louisa were left alone. Taking her hands into his, Robert came straight to the point and proposed. "Dearest Louisa, would you like to be a missionary in China? Will you then go with me?"[4] (While this sounds unromantic by today's standards, Robert was observing the convention for a proposal in his circle, that to avoid misunderstanding he should declare not only his intention but its consequences.)[5] Louisa's immediate reply "Yes!" was influenced by a recent experience of God through which she had "given herself to God, that He might use her in whatever way or place He pleased."[6] The wedding date was set for 7 September at nearby St Stephen's Church in Dublin.

Early Sketches of Robert and Louisa

The Stewart and Smyly families both rejoiced at the engagement. For generations Stewarts had been members of the Anglo-Irish gentry, their sons being educated in England at prestigious boarding schools and entering the professions. They belonged to the Protestant minority in Ireland. Robert was the seventh son of James Robert Stewart, a wealthy land agent. His paternal grandfather had been an Irish Member of the British Parliament, and his great grandfather first Baronet of County Cork. Robert's mother, Martha Eleanor Warren, was the daughter of a leading barrister.

4. Dawson, *Missionary Heroines*, 105.
5. Welch, *Flower Mountain Murders*, Pt. 1, 41 also interprets his proposal less prosaically, arguing that contemporary mission accounts generally focused on the religious rather than romantic element, though the latter was often present.
6. This was also a 'Keswick-type' experience. See further Watson, *In Life and Death*, 93, a book about the Stewarts compiled by Louisa's sister.

Robert himself was brought up in Gortleitragh House, a stately home in Dublin, and was educated at Marlborough College in Wiltshire.

The Smyly family had an even more prominent position in Dublin society. Its partriach, Josiah, had been an eminent surgeon, and its matriarch, Ellyn was founder of the The Smyly Homes and Schools, the best-known charity in the country. Two of Louisa's brothers were distinguished surgeons, and another was a Major in the British Army. A deeply religious family, the Smylys had strong connections with the Irish Church Mission which worked among the poor and needy.[7]

In June Robert returned to London and, along with Llewleyn Lloyd, was ordained deacon in St. Paul's Cathedral. Not long afterwards, he heard from CMS that the departure date for China was set for only a few days after the upcoming wedding. He and Louisa spent the next three months not only preparing for their marriage but preparing for the rest of their life in China. They were married at St. Stephen's Church (better known to Dubliners as the 'Peppercanister' due to its distinctive spire) on Thursday, 7 September. Since this looked out on to Merrion Square, Louisa was able to walk to the ceremony from her home. The service was conducted by Robert's elder brother, Henry, and the church was full with distinguished guests. Children from the Smyly Schools sent Louisa a note expressing "the love and interest" from those "she has been helpful to in Dublin."[8]

大屠殺中倖存的孩子們

The month-long sea voyage to China gave Robert and Louisa opportunity to have an extended honeymoon. Arriving in Foochow on 14 November, they were met by John and Mary Wolfe, and transported by sedan-chairs from the busy river port to the large walled city. The intoxicating mix of new sights, smells, and sounds was unlike anything they had ever experienced. After crossing the ancient Bridge of Ten Thousand Ages, they were taken along stone-paved, overcrowded streets adorned with colourful banners, through a turreted City Gate to Black Rock Hill. Wu-shi-shan, its traditional name, was crowned with a Buddhist Temple, below which were a few missionary houses and a large area of vacant ground. The hill overlooked the city of half a million people, which was bounded on two sides by the Min

---

7. Ellyn Smyly's work inspired the more widely known Barnardo Homes in various parts of the world. See further V. Smyly, *Mrs Smyly's Home*.

8. Drawing on Watson, *In Life and Death*, 157.

River, and framed by high mountains to the West where temperatures were ten degrees lower in the summer months.

The arrival of the new missionaries buoyed the spirits of the small but growing Anglican communities in both Foochow and its surrounding districts. The recent death of an up-country colleague had left the Wolfes the only CMS representatives in the province. Once Robert and Louisa had settled into their home, over the next year their main task was to learn the local dialect, a version of Hokkien different to both Mandarin and Cantonese. This was undertaken with the aid of Chinese teachers who knew only a little English. Louisa's facility with languages helped her master the complex tones more quickly than Robert, and she was soon able to begin conversing with servants, shopkeepers, and local people. As their language skills developed, they began to explore more of their new city. At the bottom of the hill was the ninth century Black Pagoda, nearby was the central Three Lanes and Seven Alleys market area, and a little further on the impressive West Lake with its acres of pavilions and cultivated gardens.

The Stewarts came to the province several decades after the Opium Wars that led to foreign nations imposing unfair trading rights upon China. Its capital was one of the Treaty Ports to which the West had access, and its Naval Yard one of the first industrial developments by the Chinese. Robert and Louisa arrived during a political program known as 'Self-Strengthening', designed by the Qing Government to lessen the one-sided nature of the treaties, and begin modernising the nation. Initially, this focussed on manufacturing military hardware and weapons, but was now shifting to raw materials and commercial products. Unfortunately, such widespread problems as shortage of capital, bureaucratic inertia, lack of coordination, and political corruption slowed industrial development. So far as religion was concerned, while the central government permitted the dissemination of Christianity, it encouraged provincial authorities to restrict its influence in all kinds of practical ways. [9]

Once Robert reached proficiency in the language, he was given two responsibilities—heading up the CMS Boys School, and developing a small theological college. His strategy was to concurrently prepare teachers for work in schools, and catechists—in reality pastors—to work in churches. Within a year, the number of theological students had doubled. Since the course included both Biblical and Chinese studies, he recruited a local Christian co-Principal, who had a degree in Chinese literature, to work with him. Robert soon realised that, if both the School and the College were to

9. On the development of China during the second half of the 19th century, see further Hsu, *Rise of Modern China*, 261–312 and, more briefly, Kerr, *Short History*, 109–111.

grow, a larger complex of buildings was needed to both teach and accommodate students. As CMS said they didn't have enough money for this, the Stewarts immediately began seeking funds from friends in Ireland.

Initially, Louisa was mainly occupied with establishing their new home and assisting in the CMS Girls School. In May 1877, the two of them were invited to be the CMS representatives of Fukien province at the triennial Conference of Protestant Missionaries held over two weeks in Shanghai. Present at this were experienced missionaries in China including Hudson Taylor. Addresses were given on a range of subjects, and delegates shared ideas and reports on their work and what was happening across the nation. There were lectures and discussions of such topics as approaches to ancestral worship, dealing with opium addiction, self-supporting native churches, women's work etc.

On 8 October, the Stewart's first child, Arthur Dudley, was born. Being away from the support of her wider family, Louisa was grateful for the presence of a good doctor, the help of an amah to assist with care of the baby and for the advice of fellow missionary wives. Over the next few months, Robert prepared the way to build the new school and college. Plans were drawn up for a complex of buildings containing individual accommodation for around fifty students, a large lecture room, dining hall, bell tower, and an office for the headmaster. After attempting to buy a block of land adjacent to the CMS compound—whose owner contracted to sell it at an agreed price, but then reneged because he wanted more money—Robert chose a small piece of ground within the compound itself. Though having the legal right to proceed, he also asked for the British Consul's consent. The Consul's only request was that Robert allay a superstitious objection by the Chinese Literati Club, whose premises were further up the hill below the Buddhist Temple, that any such buildings would bring bad luck or misfortune to residents they overlooked. Out of courtesy, Robert wrote to the Club, explaining that the buildings would be hidden from the view of the residents. Receiving no further protest from the Literati, and conscious that they watched the progress of construction but said nothing, he assumed there was no problem. He also cultivated a good rapport with local residents and found they had no objection. Only after the buildings were completed, did the Literati, inflamed by a notorious visiting agitator from Canton (now Guangzhou), demand that the Consul stop further work and demolish the construction. Having fulfilled all necessary requirements and spent a significant amount of donated money, Robert refused. This set the stage for the unexpected series of events that came to be known as the Wu-shi-shan Incident.[10]

Behind the scenes, leaders of the Literati Club hired an unruly crowd of men from outside the city to demonstrate against the new construction. Choosing the day when the city's Mandarin and a consular official were inspecting the site, on 30 August the mob broke into the new school and college, began destroying property, and set fire to the main building. The Mandarin made no protest and, when alerted to what was happening by his representative, neither did the Consul. After all the effort involved in, and money raised for, its construction, Robert was understandably devastated. Since the mob continued to raise disturbances against other mission properties in the area, the captain of a British ship that had just docked in the Min River offered to send an armed squad for protection. Convinced this would give the wrong impression of Christian work, and in any case might only inflame the situation further, Robert declined, even though this increased the risk to the lives of his family and others.

A few days later, the unruly crowd reappeared, surrounded the Stewarts' house, and issued violent threats against Robert, Louisa and the baby inside. While Arthur was too young to recall the incident, he retained a vivid memory of being told what happened.

> Our house was surrounded by a yelling crowd who tried to break in the doors and windows. Previously father, with the aid of a few faithful Chinese, had barred and secured the house which was quite strongly built and resisted the efforts of the crowd.
>
> There was a door at the back which they had not had time to secure. Looking through a chink father saw a big Chinese man holding the door closed with one hand, while with the other he hammered on it and kicked it fiercely, shouting loudly blood-thirsty threats of what he would do to the inhabitants when he got in. "Death to the foreign devils!" he shouted. Father recognised him as a staunch friend. He had known about the door, had been the first to rush to it, and, finding it open, was deliberately holding it shut, and by his size and determination prevented any other from trying to break it down. Then some friendly Chinese hurried us to a boat which lay in a nearby creek, and we were taken to the foreign settlement on the island of Nantai. God had wonderfully delivered us, but I wondered what were the feelings of mother, as she waited hour after hour,

---

10. Here we can only summarise the complex and protracted nature of this event. For key sources and interpretations, see Robert's letters in Welch, *Flower Mountain Murders*, Pt.2, 184–192; Stock, *Christ and Fukien*, 23–25; *Dublin Daily Express*, 3 and especially Carlson, *Foochow. Missionaries*, 133–170.

with her baby in her arms, while the crowd yelled and battered outside.[11]

After the situation finally settled down, the Literati brought a legal case against the presence of the Mission. They argued this on seven grounds: five of these were so specious they quickly withdrew, one was dismissed by the judge, and one controverted issue was upheld. After a delay, CMS in the UK appealed the outcome to the Chinese Government in Peking (now Beijing). This took some time to deliberate, but overruled the previous judgment and decided in CMS's favour, affirming its right to continue operations on the present site, and demanding reparation for damages. Its findings, however, were only communicated to the British Consul in Foochow who saw this as an opportunity to gain approval for a long-favoured project. Deliberately concealing the decision from the missionaries, he struck a back-door deal with officials in Peking to exchange the CMS plot for land on which a racecourse could be built outside the city walls. The Mission was asked to vacate its city compound at the end of 1880, and then given a three-month extension while discussions took place about an alternative site in the Foreign Concession on Nantai Island across the Min River. It was only many years later that this back-door deal came to light,[12] but the Chinese officials did grant $3000 in compensation for the destroyed buildings and, despite objections by the Literati, offered rental of a site on the Island as a replacement.

A few people at the time criticised Robert for his handling of the whole matter. They felt he had acted in a rather distant manner. Others defended him, pointing out that he had fulfilled, even exceeded, the formal requirements, had sought to consult with key stakeholders, and had the support of Chinese living nearby. Roberts believed he had done the right thing—legally, politically and culturally—and was ultimately exonerated. If he had erred, it was underestimating the strength of the Literati's antagonism to anything Western, the importance of building strategic relationships with potential opponents, and the lawless and volatile character of some elements among the Chinese population. This was due to his being relatively new to the culture, but even taking these steps might not have prevented the disturbance occurring. Robert and Louisa learned a great deal from this experience that would influence their future work, especially their approach to potentially violent opposition.

On 27 March 1879, Louisa gave birth to a second son, Philip Smyly, whom the Chinese called 'Pelik'. Now, with two small children under eighteen months, it became necessary to have the help of two amahs (or

---

11. A. Stewart, *After Seventy Years*, 6.
12. On this see Stock, *For Christ and Fukien*, 24–25.

nannies) so she could be freed up to develop a School for Bible-women which prepared them for evangelistic work in the city and nearby districts. Meanwhile Robert found temporary rented accommodation for his school and theological students. Their son Arthur later recounted his memories of family life at this time.

> I see a boy of two, climbing on a dining table. On it is a cup containing what looks like custard. Unfortunately, the initial letter is 'm' not 'c', and . . . Mother appearing in answer to loud shrieks, saw a small figure yelling blue murder with trickles of mustard out of the corners of his mouth.
> I saw a small figure standing before Mother and an accusing voice saying, "Arthur, did you eat the fruit I told you not to eat?" "No, mummy, I didn't." "Then what are those red marks on your mouth?" Back came the quick reply, "Mummy, the mosquitoes were biting me." It is regretful to add that the servants were delighted—"such a clever baby."
>
> A more pleasing picture is that of a small boy, about three years old, going up to the little mother, who was very disconsolate because father had gone up-country on one of his itinerating tours, and saying to her "Don't cry mummy. I can take care of you," and then the little figure strutted away shouting orders to the servants, and they, with understanding smiles, hastened to obey. "You're always a great help to me, darling," Louisa replied.[13]

Their third son, James Robert, named after his paternal grandfather, was born on 7 January, 1881. From the beginning he was a sickly child, and suffered respiratory problems because of the humidity in Foochow. Relocating the Mission across the Min River to the Cangshan District on Nantai Island took some time. Along with new premises for the CMS Boys and Girls boarding schools, residences for three missionary families had to be built. Robert was also responsible for oversight of the numerous Day Schools in the city.[14] Nantai Island was where the majority of Westerners worked and lived. Some were diplomatic staff, some were involved in the tea, silk and other trades, and some were attached to missionary societies. This area, outside the walled city, had once been Foochow's cemetery, and was believed to

---

13. A. Stewart, After Seventy Years, 2.

14. These were set up in a variety of premises, largely staffed by local teachers, and supervised by a missionary who made occasional visits. At the time in the province of Fukien, there were approximately one hundred mission stations, some with a school, church and dispensary.

be full of ghosts. Consequently, their presence and residence encountered little interference from those opposed to the presence of foreigners.

For the three small boys, life on Nantai initially made little difference, though they did enjoy an occasional trip to Sharp Peak, at the mouth of the Min River, where they were able to paddle in the sea. From an early age the children were exposed to the local dialect as well as to the common maladies. As Arthur recalls:

> I learned to speak Chinese . . . before I could speak English . . . I sometimes corrected mother for mistakes in tones . . . [There was a] continual struggle against illness in those days, and soon the dreaded malaria had me in its grip. There was little knowledge of quinine, and all that mother could do was to put me in a warm bath, slowly adding cold water, to bring my temperature down. But this could not go on for long. To save my life the doctor ordered that I and my brother Philip should be sent to England, or rather Ireland, as it happened.[15]

大屠殺中倖存的孩子們

One of the missionaries the Stewarts knew well, Margaret Foster, was about to leave on furlough and, providentially, offered to take the two older boys, with the help of an amah, to Ireland. "So, one afternoon, Mother took her two boys in a launch down the river Min to the coastal steamer . . . and when evening began to fall, put them to bed in a strange bedroom, joined them in their baby prayers, waited till they had fallen asleep, and then with a heartache which can only be guessed, went back to the work that needed her."[16] The ship took them via Hong Kong, where they stayed for a few days at St Paul's College which, though Arthur did not know it at the time, was to be the site of his future home and work.

---

15. A. Stewart, *After Seventy Years*, 3.

16. A. Stewart, *After Seventy Years*, 3. Margaret Foster ultimately came to Australia with her husband, George Fagg, ran an orphanage, and was involved in sending many missionaries to China.

An Irish Family in the East (1875–1895)

Gortleitragh in Black Rock, Dublin

The voyage back to England took a month.

> I remember little of the voyage except that the amah spoke no English and frequently asked me to translate for her. One day she wanted to ask the steward for soap. I told her 'sugar' and watched the resultant impasse with pleasure. Miss Foster took us over to Ireland where we were to make our home at Gortleitragh, Kingston, the residence of our grandfather, James Robert Stewart, looked after by his daughter Emily (Aunt Tem, as she was known).[17]

With new missionary residences completed on Nantai, and construction of the Girls and Boys Schools under way, Robert was eager to build the theological college. Though the City Council provided a grant to fund this, the land allocated on Nantai turned out to be too small for an additional building. As it took some time to find an appropriate site, it was not until 1883 that the building was completed. Robert decided to name it Trinity College after his alma mater in Dublin. It was officially opened by Bishop Burden during his visit from the Diocesan headquarters in Hong Kong. Though still without a permanent base, Louisa continued to develop the

---

17. A. Stewart, *After Seventy Years*, 2.

training of Bible-women who came from the city and nearby districts for a three-month course in bible knowledge and evangelism. Along with this, she had begun cultivating work among the wives of Chinese merchants and officials in the capital, many of whom were foot-bound and largely restricted to home. This ministry took the form of a hostess inviting other women from her social class to meet an 'exotic' foreigner and hear about her way of life, customs and beliefs.

Finally, on 4 September 1882, the Stewarts had their first little girl, Mildred Eleanor. From the beginning she was an active, robust child, who thrived on the attention of her parents and amahs. By contrast, James's health continued to cause concern. In Dublin, the two boys took a while to settle into their new way of life. As Arthur wrote:

> Our first game was to sit on the path and pile up the gravel in the shape of Chinese graves, so familiar to us. One day Miss Foster remarked to Tem that it was a good thing she could not understand what we were saying, for we were, in all ignorance, using horrible swear words picked up by us from Chinese coolies ... Poor Tem must have had a difficult time with us, for we were not only shy but extremely nervous and delicate—due to malaria, the noises of a Chinese city, and idol processions. Some years later, when father brought home some idols, we were terrified and fled shrieking.[18]

On 29 April 1884, another daughter, Kathleen Louisa, was born. Despite having her mother's name, she looked very much like her father, and was a great companion for her older sister. By now, Louisa had made the family home a well-known haven of hospitality. On his first visit, a new missionary Dr van Someren wrote "All of a sudden a door opened ... and a woman came out, a bright light behind her, holding an infant in her arms ... I thought she was an angel', and added, 'and I have not changed my mind.'"[19]

Around this time, James unfortunately contracted malaria, and the Stewarts were advised that his generally poor health required specialist medical attention only available in the United Kingdom [UK]. Knowing that within a year they would be returning for their first furlough, Robert and Louisa reluctantly decided James should join the other children in Ireland.

---

18. A. Stewart, After Seventy Years, 4.
19. A. Stewart, After Seventy Years, 2.

In the interim, life for the boys in Gortleitragh was quite a contrast. This stately mansion, set on a large estate, was in the coastal village of Kingston on the fringe of Dublin.[20]

> [It] was a place full of people. The row of servants looked imposing as they filed in each morning for prayers, led by 'Old William' the butler . . .grandfather was a very handsome old gentleman who seldom spoke to 'the children' but was wonderfully polite to his two daughters. Besides grandfather, Gortleitragh was the home of aunts, Emily and Florence. The latter was very young and . . . wonderfully musical. What music we had in those days with many guests in the drawing room listening to old time duets! . . . There seemed to be unending numbers of visitors, for in addition to music, there was the attraction of four excellent tennis courts and a racquet court.[21]

When James arrived, the other two boys initially looked on him as something abnormal, since he still spoke Chinese more than English, and they had long forgotten theirs. They were always excited to see Chinese stamps on letters that arrived, knowing that they were from their parents, especially their mother. These not only shared family news that kept them in touch with their sisters but reminded them of how much they were prayed for and loved.

When Robert, Louisa, and the girls eventually arrived in Dublin, Arthur records:

> I well remember our excitement. We were also to see our sisters, Mildred and Kathleen, and I remember the thrill when I heard Kathleen's shrill baby voice for the first time. We were close friends from the start . . . Father stands out as one who encouraged our physical side. He built us a trapeze and parallel bars, and taught us to use them . . . Mother moves in a shadowy way . . . leaving a trail of sweetness and love.[22]

After eight strenuous years away, furlough back in Dublin provided time not only to regain their full strength but opportunity to be a whole family again. Robert and Louisa were also keen to stimulate more interest in the needs of China. He focussed on stirring up interest in their province among students and graduates at Trinity College. An address he gave there

---

20. This property was the home of the German Ambassador to Ireland during World War II, the place where the Irish Prime President de Valera expressed his condolences on the death of Hitler, and later the Irish Free State Governor-General's residence.
21. A. Stewart, *After Seventy Years*, 4–5.
22. A. Stewart, *After Seventy Years*, 5–6.

touched a number of young men willing to serve in China.[23] This led to the founding of the Dublin University Fukien Mission [DUFM], and its first candidate, J. Stratford Collins, began missionary training. Louisa focussed on challenging women to work in China. Up till now, CMS only accepted the wives, or widows, of missionaries for overseas service. Through the work of Margaret Foster since her return to Ireland, Louisa heard that a number of single women were willing to offer themselves for missionary service. Since CMS was still procrastinating about sending unmarried women, she turned to the Church of England Zenana Missionary Society [CEZMS] which had previously only worked in India, for help. It readily agreed, and two sisters, Innie and Hessie Newcombe, began preparing to serve in Fukien.

While all this was happening, the Stewarts heard that the outbreak of naval hostilities between the French and the Chinese which had begun before they left, was severely disrupting mission work in Fukien. In some places, strong anti-foreign feeling led to some converts being persecuted. Robert and Louisa were naturally concerned for their students and other local Christians in the province.

Before returning to China, difficult decisions had to be made about the children's education. Reluctantly, like almost all missionary families at the time, Robert and Louisa realized that their older children would be at a distinct educational disadvantage if they went back with them.[24] This was not yet an issue for the girls, who were still pre-schoolers. Though separation from the boys would be painful, it seemed to be the most loving option, and was the choice made by virtually all missionary couples. The wider family was fully in agreement with this decision and offered its support. Aunt Tem was willing to continue providing a home for them, and uncle George offered to act as their guardian.

大屠殺中倖存的孩子們

At the start of 1886, the Stewarts returned to their work on Nantai Island. Within a year, however, Robert was diagnosed with malaria, gastric ulcers and dysentery, which frequently left him exhausted and in pain. Attempts to control this by taking an extended six-week break in the cooler mountain

---

23. Patrick Comerford, "Dublin Family."

24. For an example of missionary attitudes at the time, see MacGillivray, *China Mission Year Book*. Appendix, xl. Though he acknowledges that most boys in well-to-do circles were sent off to boarding schools in Ireland, William Smyly, 'Irish Family in the East', pt.4 does not explain why most missionaries felt the need to take this step.

climate of Kuliang (now Guliang) failed to make much difference.[25] So in early 1888, when his condition deteriorated further, the CMS doctor insisted that they should return to Ireland for more specialised treatment. Robert was in such a poor state that many thought he might never be well enough to work again. The Mission asked Llewelyn Lloyd and his wife Sarah to take over Robert's work in the theological college and Louisa's in the Bible-women's training school. On arriving back at Gortleitragh, Louisa's brother Dr Philip Smyly ordered a range of tests and complete bed rest. Aided by medication, in mid-summer Robert was well enough to go on holidays to Wales with the family. Realising she would need extra help with the children, Louisa employed thirteen-year old Helena Yallop, or Lena as she was known, from the Smyly Homes as their nanny.

Even though Robert's health kept improving after the holiday, the doctor's advice was to spend the winter in a milder climate. The Stewarts decided that if Lena would become a permanent member of the household and help look after the girls, Robert, Louisa and the boys could go to southern Europe where the weather would be warmer. They sailed on the *SS Malta* to the Italian Riviera, staying mostly in half-empty hotels and pensions, and then travelled on to France.

> Mother spoke French well, but father frequently lapsed into fluent Fukienese, much to the amazement of porters and waiters. We learned to roller-skate there . . . father [was] a truly good companion; games in which he joined always went with a swing and there were no walks like those he took with us—cross-country rambles full of adventure, with the possibility of an angry-farmer coming to ask what we were doing—not that any farmer could be angry with father for long.[26]

The family travelled to Lourdes, which was full of pilgrims, then Bourdeaux, before returning home.

On 1 August 1889, their fourth son, Herbert Norman, was born. Shortly afterwards, as Robert had been appointed to CMS's Deputation Staff in England, the family moved to Bedford, which was easily accessible by train to the Mission's headquarters in London. The three older boys started at Bedford Grammar School. By now, Robert was well enough to recommence his translation of the New Testament into the Romanised, or

---

25. The Annual CMS Conference, discussing administrative matters, and CMS Convention, following a Keswick-style program, were held at Kuliang in the mountains above Foochow in late July, after which missionaries took a four to six week break from their work during the height of the summer heat.

26. A. Stewart, After Seventy Years, 5.

alphabetic, form of the local dialect.[27] This was his contribution to a long-term project designed to make the Bible more accessible to illiterate men and women in all CMS' educational institutions in the province. Louisa began undertaking deputation work to raise financial support for the work of women missionaries. According to Dr Eugene Stock, Editorial Secretary of CMS: "She was even more powerful a speaker than her husband. I have been with her at a drawing-room meeting, appointed to speak after her, and when she sat down felt that any other address would only mar the effect of her loving, moving, burning words: and I have risen and simply said, 'I will not add a syllable.'"[28]

With another Dublin winter approaching, the family was again advised to spend a few months in a warmer climate. This time the whole family went by ferry to the seaside town of Niton on the Isle of Wight, close to the popular health resort of Ventnor. During the school term, the boys were able to continue their education at a nearby school and Louisa taught the girls at home. On their return, Robert felt well enough to begin doing regular deputation work for CMS. Before long he was receiving more invitations to speak in different parts of the UK than he could handle. On occasions, when this travel was being discussed at family meals, the children would sing a chorus they had learned from him: "Have courage, my boy, have courage my boy, have courage my boy, to say No!"

From the home base in Bedford, Louisa was also involved in organising a deputation tour by Mrs Diyong Ahok from Foochow. The wife of a wealthy Christian merchant, Mrs Ahok had come to faith a few years earlier through visits to her home by female missionaries. Margaret Foster and Louisa had also befriended her. She was coming to the UK to challenge young single women about God's call to China. In spring 1890, Louisa welcomed Mrs Ahok and her maid to London. Acting as their interpreter, over several weeks she went with them to more than one hundred meetings around England and Ireland. One such widely-attended event was held at the Royal Pavilion in Brighton, with another on the beach near Brighton Pier.

---

27. In contrast to learning more than five thousand characters, each of which stood for a word, the alphabetic version had only around two dozen consonants, and four diacritic tones, to build the same vocabulary.

28. Dawson, *Missionary Heroines*, 118–19.

An Irish Family in the East (1875–1895)

Louisa and Robert with Mrs Ahok

Having been bound from birth, Mrs Ahok's feet were so tiny—less than three inches long—that she had to sit in a chair whenever she spoke. At one meeting, seeing "interested faces and sympathetic tears", she said "I am glad you feel for my people who are without God; but that is not enough. Think before you leave your seats what you will do for China. We have a Chinese proverb—"when the stove is hot, put in the cakes." Of Louisa it was reported that: "The interpretation was so clearly spoken and in her usual quiet voice, yet she was heard at the furthest end. Many remarked afterwards with what ease she interpreted each sentence as Mrs Ahok spoke . . . Her beautiful simplicity of character, her self-forgetfulness and unobtrusiveness were remarkable."[29] Mrs Ahok's visit highlighted the importance of women go-

---

29. Watson, *In Life and Death*, 166, 143. See further *Behind the Great Wall*, 60–90, Louisa Stewart, *Women's Work in Fuh-kien*, and, more fully, Margaret Fagg, *Two Golden Lilies*. This was the married name of Margaret Foster, mentioned earlier.

ing to China as missionaries and challenged those at home to pray for and support their work. Sadly, while she was returning home via Canada, Mrs Ahok received a telegram saying that her husband had unexpectedly died. Despite criticism from family in Foochow that his death was punishment for deserting the Chinese gods, she continued to give herself to reaching women with the Gospel.

During Louisa's deputations the two girls, Mil and Kat as they were called, enjoyed spending time with their nanny Lena while the boys were at school. One of her letters to a friend recalls the seven and five-year old: "acting like coolies, load bearers, trying to imitate everything they say, carrying on conversation in make-believe Chinese, with long pipes in their mouths."[30] Overall, life at 7 Welbeck Ave. was working out really well for everyone. Though Robert was often away on deputation, he ensured that time was kept free for such children's activities as boating on the river Ouse, skating on it when it was frozen, and tobogganing in a home-made cart. Both parents took the family on visits to Bedford's historic castle and the gaol where John Bunyan had written his influential *Pilgrims Progress*.

> Daily prayers were a central feature of family life. There was nothing stuffy or formal. First there was a hymn, then a short reading with questions and explanations, and finally an extempore prayer. A hymn they particularly enjoyed was "Bringing in the Sheaves", which they parodied as "Bringing in the Chinese"! On Sunday afternoons, when Robert was away, a favourite activity was Louisa taking the children to the river bank, reading a book like *The Last Days of Pompeii* in such a way that kept even the youngest entertained. Looking back on this time, Arthur wrote: "I can see how God used father's illness for our good and much other good that followed from the years he was kept in England as a result of his illness".[31]

As part of his CMS duties, in June 1891, Robert attended the annual Keswick Convention in the Lake District. This large interdenominational gathering had become the premier event for those considering missionary service. For Robert it was an opportunity to reconnect with men like Evan Hopkins, missionaries on furlough from China, and others from his training days in Islington. For him a highlight was learning a new hymn 'In the Secret of His Presence', which captured the renewed intimacy with God that he experienced during the Convention. On his return home, Robert taught it to the rest of the family and they sang it together every day for weeks.

---

30. On Helena Yellop, see Welch, *Flower Mountain Murders*, Pt. 2.12.
31. A. Stewart, After Seventy Years, 7.

An Irish Family in the East (1875–1895)

A few months later, Dr Eugene Stock received an invitation from Australia for an experienced missionary to speak at rallies in several States from April 1892. The visit, including the return voyage and a side-trip to New Zealand, would last around several months. A few weeks before the scheduled departure the invited speaker unexpectedly withdrew. Stock immediately thought of Robert Stewart and asked him to be the substitute. As Louisa was shortly due to have their seventh child, Robert's inclination was to say no. But she saw this as a God-given opportunity to challenge Australian women for missionary service in China. Since the Stewarts were hoping to return to China the following year, Louisa felt this trip would be a good test of Robert's health and that with Lena and extra servant help she could manage without him.

Robert with Chinese exhibits in Australia

Three weeks into the voyage Robert received a telegram saying that Louisa had given birth to a son, Evan George, and that all was well at home.

Arriving in Melbourne on Sunday 24 April, that very evening he spoke at an Anglican Church where two young sisters, Eleanor and Harriet Saunders, offered to go to join their work in China. Over the next few months, Robert travelled large distances to speak at meetings in metropolitan and country areas, in both Victoria and New South Wales. In his descriptions of China, Robert would explain that although:

> There now nearly 100,000 believers in a land of 400 million, there was still only one missionary for every 250,000 people. He held a graven figure up in his hand, and described how families in every house prayed to idols like this for protection. He showed them a very small shoe, and explained how infant girls were cruelly hurt and deformed by foot-binding. He told of the towers outside cities containing a small hole and pit into which new born girls were frequently cast.[32]

So effective was Robert's visit to Australia, that a number of young women began applying for overseas service, especially to China[33]; many clergy and parishioners were challenged to support missionary work; and what up till now were mere branches of CMS UK were turned into independent State Associations. As the Archbishop of Sydney later concluded, "in the light of the years that have followed [it was] momentous for the whole missionary life of the church in Australia."[34]

During Robert's time away, Louisa continued to make contact with women who were interested in going to China as missionaries. In May 1892, she invited a young Irish woman, Amy Carmichael, to stay in Bedford. As they talked, it was almost settled that Amy would travel to Fukien with the Stewarts later that year. However, on 16 July, in the margin of her *Daily Light*, Amy noted that Mrs Stewart had written to say that the return trip to China had to be delayed. (Presumably this was because Robert's successful time away had been extended). Believing that she shouldn't postpone beginning her work, Amy was accepted by CMS for Japan instead. She never forgot, however, that her life would have had a very different outcome if she waited to go with the Stewarts to China.[35] While Robert was speaking in

---

32. See further Banks & Banks, *The Faraway Pagoda*, 21

33. Among these were two of our forebears, Sophie Sackville Newton and Amy Oxley Wilkinson, whose stories we have told in our books *The Faraway Pagoda*, and *They Shall See His Face*, respectively.

34. *Church Missionary Review*, June 1913, 353.

35. Houghton, *Amy Carmichael of Dohnavur*, 1953, 6. Amy went on to become one of the 20th century's best-known missionaries for her work in rescuing and caring for orphans in India.

New Zealand on the last leg of his trip, Arthur, now almost fifteen, began as a boarder at Haileybury College in Hertfordshire. This major private school had been carefully selected for the education of the three older boys. Arriving home in mid-December, the whole family looked forward to spending Christmas together. On the day itself, returning home from church, the children were delighted to find some interesting gifts from Australia under their beautifully decorated tree. After dinner, they sang some favourite carols, accompanied by their mother on the piano and father playing his cornet. Little did they know that this was to be their last Christmas together.

大屠殺中倖存的孩子們

Early in 1893, official confirmation finally came from CMS about their return to China.

As their work in the Foochow was now in good hands, Robert was appointed Superintendent of the largest rural mission district in the province, ninety miles to the north-west of the capital. Its compound and headquarters outside the regional center of Kucheng (now Gutian), contained boys and girls boarding schools, an orphanage, a dispensary, and two missionary residences. Nearby was a leper settlement and, in the surrounding villages, several mission outposts and two dozen day schools. Staffing for this work was largely carried on by women from CEZMS, a number of whom had gone to China because of the Stewarts.

The success of Robert's time in Australasia convinced CMS in London to ask the Stewarts whether *en route* to China they would make a similar visit to Canada. Though excited by this possibility, Robert and Louisa felt it would be too much for the children. But Lena, now very much part of the family, volunteered to take the girls and two younger boys with her by ship to Foochow. Realising that Mildred, now eleven, would be a great help, Louisa gratefully accepted their offer.

The time in Canada led to a greater interest in missionary work in China, and to the first Canadian woman applying to serve there. Church Missionary Associations similar to those set up a year earlier in Australia and New Zealand were also established.[36] Louisa's sister Mary was among those farewelling her nieces and nephews on the first leg of their long voyage: "How vividly we remember the start that October evening, the little travellers well wrapped up for their night journey, dear little four-year-old

---

36. See the Anglican Church of Canada website at anglican.ca.

Herbert clinging to a stuffed calico 'pussy'; and Lena moving about among them, so quiet and self-possessed.[37]

Herbert and Evan before trip

In early November, Lena and the children reached Hong Kong and changed ships for Foochow. There they linked up with the Saunders sisters from Melbourne, who were joining the mission in Kucheng. Landing at Nantai Island three days later, they were to stay at 'The Olives', the CEZMS Mission House, until Robert and Louisa's arrival in a month's time. While they were waiting, Lena and the children were shown around some of the sights in the city. For her, everything was new and strange, while for the two girls it was a reintroduction to the life and language of their earlier years. Meeting their parents on the wharf was a joyous reunion. It took a week to organise transport and porters for the hundred-mile, three-day inland trip. This began with a boat trip, including an overnight stay, up the expansive Min River, to the little port of Coi-kau, followed by a full day's walk and ride in sedan-chairs along a steep mountainous track to their destination. It was dark when they finally arrived at the Mission Station just outside the walls of the city. Waking early the next morning and pulling back the curtains, Louisa was overcome by the beauty of the vista before her—an ancient walled city, with a clear mountain stream at one edge, surrounded by towering mountains. Robert remarked that they could have searched

---

37. Cited in Watson, *In Life and Death*, 160.

the world over and not found a more beautiful location than that which God had chosen for them.[38] Settling in just a few days before Christmas, the Stewarts couldn't but help remember the contrast between this and their last Christmas with the older boys in Bedford.

Assisting the missionaries in a district the size of modern-day Israel were over thirty male catechists serving small village churches and engaged in local evangelism. Believing that China could never be reached except through its own people, from the start Robert gave top priority to encouraging and training such workers. This made him "one of those pioneering the systematic, selective training of catechists with the intention of creating an educated, self-supporting network of Bible teachers and church leaders."[39] As the main CMS representative, he also liaised with the American Methodists Mission working in the area, and sought to build good relationships with the Mandarin, magistrates, and public officials in the city.

Louisa's main responsibility was to provide pastoral help and encouragement to around a dozen or so female missionaries who came and went from their posts in the district, and to develop the on-site training of Chinese Bible-women for evangelism in the villages. When Robert was itinerating, she also had to oversee the day-to-day running of the mission compound. The couple soon saw the need to grow the Mission's work, extending the size of the 'Birds Nest'[40] baby orphanage, doubling the number of day schools, and developing the Bible-women's training school. This required additional funding, for which they appealed to their network of friends and family in Ireland. Robert and Louisa often gave their own money to local people who suffered a loss or tragedy when none of their fellow-countrymen were willing to help. They financed the purchase of two cottages in Hwasang in the hills above Kucheng, one for their family and one for other missionaries, as a place for retreat in the summer.

The Stewarts believed that, as far as possible, adapting to the local culture was crucial for all their missionaries. As far as possible this meant eating, dressing, relating, even designing buildings, like their Chinese neighbors. Implementing this policy unfortunately brought them into conflict with some other CMS missionaries in the province, especially Archdeacon Wolfe in Foochow. According to Dr van Someren, who knew Robert well, "He was always ready to listen to the Chinese, whether he were a student or a poor village Christian. No matter what he was doing, no matter how tired

---

38. Watson, *In Life and Death*, 126.

39. A comment by C Starr in Wickeri, *Christian Encounters with Chinese Culture*, 95.

40. This was named after the Smyly Orphanage in Dublin.

he was, he would lay down his pen or book, invite his guest to be seated, and give himself up to him. No wonder that by doing so he won his way to many a heart."[41] Another missionary who stayed with the Stewarts for a while observed that their home " . . . was indeed a happy one; anything like friction among the missionaries being unknown." Louisa herself "had a peculiarly sympathetic nature, which made her a real mother [to the single women] in Kucheng; she seemed so essentially to make her own the troubles of another . . . I never heard a Christian, native or foreigner, say one word against Mrs. Stewart."[42]

On 24 June 1894, Louisa gave birth to their third daughter, Hilda Sylvia. Her sisters, Mildred almost twelve and Kathleen, ten, enjoyed 'mothering' her. Having Nellie and Topsy Saunders living in their home as governesses was not just interesting but fun. A favourite 'field trip' for Mildred was visiting Flora Codrington in her mission center, with an overnight stay at a rustic Chinese inn. Some afternoons Kathleen helped Ada Nisbet at the Bird's Nest orphanage, teaching songs and games to the children. The younger boys especially enjoyed following their father's advice for consuming unfamiliar Chinese food: "put the slugs into your mouth, swallow them as quickly as possible, and say 'Amen'!" After dinner some evenings, all four children loved seeing their father: "parade around the house in a huge pith helmet" and hearing "the melodious sound of his cornet, playing hymn tunes".[43]

In August, while the missionaries were having their first summer break in Hwasang, they began to hear reports of disturbances by a rebel society in the district. The *Chi-ih-t-sai Ti* was primarily opposed to the Imperial Dynasty in Peking, its representatives in the Province, and local authorities like the Mandarin. Because all these tolerated Western influence, the group believed that Chinese people were being drawn away from their traditional religion and values. Since missionaries were involved in this, the society was also opposed to their presence.[44]

Over the next six months, Robert heard about attacks by isolated groups of *Chi-ih-t-sai Ti* (or, because of their food preferences, 'Vegetarians' as Westerners called them) not only on villagers in various places but sometimes specifically targeting Christians. A rural church in the district was demolished and a young wife in a bible-women's class was kidnapped. After Chinese New Year in 1895, a Japanese naval blockade of Foochow led

41. Watson, *In Life and Death*, 96.
42. Welch, *Flower Mountain Murders*, Pt.2, 248.
43. These two quotes are from Berry, *Sister Martyrs of Kucheng*, 12 and 38–39.
44. See, in particular, Welch, "The Vegetarians".

to the withdrawal of a small number of soldiers protecting Kucheng. This action propelled the gathering of three thousand Vegetarians to attack the city, overturn the Mandarin, and take control of the district. The Stewarts immediately realised how menacing this could be for missionaries and their converts in the region. On hearing about the danger, Mildred and Kathleen were now old enough to be frightened not only for themselves but for their younger brothers and the new baby. Robert and Louisa wondered whether this potential threat might lead to a repeat, on a much larger scale, of what happened at Wu-Shi-shan?

2

Finding a Place in the World (1895–1905)

EARLY MORNING ON 27 March 1895, preparations were under way to celebrate Evan's third birthday, when, as young Lena wrote,

> Two of the leading Catechists came with the news that the Mandarin had, during the night, locked up the city gates, having had private information that the Vegetarians were mustering in thousands quite near, and about to march on Kucheng. They had taken their families out of the city. Those in the surrounding villages having anything to lose had entered it for protection.
>
> At six o'clock I went in to take baby, and Mrs Stewart said, "We may have to flee to Foochow." I did not hear any reason, but dressed the children. They were not surprised at being up early, as their father was to have started for the country. When they were at breakfast I put blankets and a change in each basket. The plan was to go up to Hwasang for a few days in the hope that the excitement would blow over.
>
> In the meantime, the boys, girls, women and babies [in the schools and orphanage] were hurried away, some to their homes, and the remainder to the chapel in the city. As we were anxiously watching the heavy rain, and wondering would the babies escape cold after a five hours' ride in baskets, a man came with the Mandarin's card and a polite invitation to go into the city, as he could not offer protection outside. An empty American house was placed at our disposal. The people in the fields were asking, "Why are you escaping? You need not fear."

> The boys were in their glory, being pulled up the ladder in baskets. We only had the things with us that I put up for Hwasang . . . The weather picked up, and we had two enjoyable days—like playing siege. We could see the squad of soldiers passing by with their marshal strut and weapons of the primitive type. The American doctor said he did not like the tone of the people, and that there were enough malcontents in the city who would sympathise with the invaders . . .
>
> Mr Stewart decided we must start for Foochow. The gates were blocked up. While our chairs were waiting outside, men came around asking friendly questions; the children always draw people. At the wall there was great commotion . . . the owner of the ladder wanted Mr Stewart to give him money. It ended by the ladder being pulled away. A bit of one was secured; Mr S and a man resting it against their shoulders till all the party descended.
>
> We stayed the night in the chapel at Co-yong. The morrow was Sunday . . . on the way we had a fight with the coolies . . . I had baby starting: she was crying for her mother. The coolies refused to carry Mrs Stewart if she sat in the chair with her. My coolies would not let me go. [One of the missionaries] exhorted them in the loudest terms . . . I went to the head man, whom I always found civil; all in vain, they were quite changed. I learned afterwards that Mrs Stewart had to offer extra money if they hurried quickly. The landing place was reached about five o'clock. I wish I could picture the scene for you. Crowds of curious but friendly men, as usual, asking questions . . . Just then a piece of paper was handed in . . . Mr Stewart had scribbled "Gates are open, peace is declared, all may return."[1]

Not long after their return a message came from the British Consul ordering all missionaries to proceed to Foochow until the disturbance had passed. Robert, however, felt a responsibility to stay in case the local Christians were threatened. He decided to try and arrange a meeting with the Vegetarian leader and, through some rebel sympathisers in the city, was able to organise this. To his relief, Stewart found him more moderate than some of his followers, and opposed to violence against missionaries. Over the next two months, Robert sent regular reports on the rebel situation in the district to both British and American consular officials in the capital. When it was clear that conditions were safe for missionary work to continue, the Stewart family returned.

---

1. Barnes, *Behind the Great Wall*, 164–166.

By early July, the heat in Kucheng had become stifling. Though it was still two weeks before their summer break, Louisa asked Lena to escort the children up to their summer house in Hwasang while she and the other missionaries completed their work for the year. Louisa and the rest of the group then started on their journey up the mountain.

> We got up early to send off our loads before the sun got very hot . . . and we . . .decided to walk all the way, twelve miles . . . We got in about ten o'clock and found the little girls still up watching for us . . .
>
> A new room built on to the house this year is a great improvement. It makes a fine big nursery, and the former little nursery we have given to Nellie and Topsy Saunders, so we have a large family! In the house next door we have Hessie Newcombe, Flora Codrington, Lucy Stewart [no relative]; and two others are coming shortly, Elsie Marshall and Annie Gordon . . .
>
> We are feeling much the better for our change to this cool place—not one ill . . . It is such a pretty place too. We spend our days very quietly; we have to stay indoors till 5 o'clock, and we spend the time at lessons, reading aloud, writing letters, and looking after the children. From 5 to 7 o'clock all who are inclined go for a walk, and the sisters from the other house join us. Some days they go to the village and talk to the women, and twice a week come here for prayer and Bible-reading. Sundays, Robert and I go to the village and have a sort of informal service . . .
>
> The two little boys are very well just now. Herbert is growing much stronger than he was; just at this moment they are together in a swing we had put up in the verandah. Evan sits in the middle of the seat and Herbert stands with one foot on each side of him, and works the swing up ever so high. They scream so loudly with delight that Lena has to rush out to hush them every now and then, to let baby sleep.[2]

During their Keswick Conference in the last week of July, the missionaries met for devotional talks, Bible studies, hymn singing and prayer. The main theme chosen in England for the week was 'Battles in the Old Testament', with the final session on 'Jesus' Transfiguration on the Mount' shortly before his death. The group closed its time together with a prayer of

---

2. Louisa Stewart, *Letters*, 6 and 19 July 1895 in Watson, *In Life and Death*, 127–130.

Finding a Place in the World (1895–1905)

dedication to "present ourselves, our souls and bodies, to be a reasonable and holy and living sacrifice to God."³

Summer Mission houses in Hwasang

Unknown to the missionaries, during that week an influential Vegetarian agitator from outside the district organised a coup to displace its local leader. He insisted the society make up for its failure to capture Kucheng by carrying out a decisive attack in the vicinity. After three options were discussed, lots were cast and fell on the small group at Hwasang. Around a hundred members armed themselves with swords, lances and farming implements, then set off. Though the former leader tried to warn Robert Stewart of the attack, his message failed to get through in time.

Kathleen, just eleven at the time, recounts the fateful events of Thursday 1 August.⁴

---

3. This was a paraphrase of Rom 12:1 (KJV).

4. This is drawn from an account Kathleen gave to a newspaper in Foochow a few days after the event, augmented in only a few details from incidental comments she made elsewhere. It is reproduced in Welch, *Flower Mountain Murders*, Pt 8, 853–854. For a fuller account of the background, description, and aftermath of the incident see Banks & Banks, *Valley of the Shadow*, 11–22. The first report of the incident with photos was in the *London Illustrated News*, April 17, 1895, 3–4.

Between 6.30 and 7am, Mildred and I were in the garden [outside the house] picking ferns and flowers because it was Herbert's birthday and we were going to decorate the breakfast table. We saw men coming along and at first I thought they were load-men or dang-dangs. Milly saw their spears and told me to run but I was so frightened I lay in the grass thinking perhaps they would not see me. The men did see me and took hold of me and pulled me by my hair towards the house. Just as we arrived there I fell down. They then began beating me. I got away from them and ran into the house through the back door. I tried to shut it but could not at first because the men put their sticks in. I afterwards succeeded and bolted it.

Then I went into our bedroom and got under the bed. (Entering the house through the front door, the attackers went into the parents' bedroom where they savagely hacked to death first their mother, and then father who was desperately trying to protect her.) Milly whispered "If I also get under the bed, the men will know there is somebody here, because the door is locked; I will unlock the door and lie on the bed, perhaps they will see me and not look under the bed for any others." Soon the men broke open the door and entered our bedroom. First, they pulled off all the bed clothes, opened the drawers and took what they wanted to, smashed windows and things, then began beating Mildred and cut her with their swords; afterwards they left the room. One man saw me under the bed as they were going out and gave me a knock on the head with a stick.

We next saw Topsy Saunders with her cheek very much cut, being walked backwards and forwards by the men who were asking her questions, and if not answered quickly dug a spear into her. One question we heard them ask was about her money and she told them they had taken all she had... Next we saw Nellie Saunders lying by the bedroom door moaning (and writhing from a fatal spear wound.) From the window we saw men outside the back door beating and killing the other missionary ladies. Four were outside, one women's head I saw quite smashed up in a corner, it was an awful sight.

Very soon I heard a rushing noise like water, went out to see what it was and found our house on fire. I went back to Mildred and told her and she got up and we walked through the servant's rooms to the nursery where we found Herbert covered with blood, Lena lying on the ground with baby beside her and Evan sitting (in his cot) crying. I screamed at Lena. She did not answer; I tried to lift her up but could not. I took baby first and laid her down outside, then went back for Evan. We then all (including Mildred and Herbert) went down past the ladies' house, which was also in a blaze, into the little wood.

After waiting there a little while I saw Miss Codrington with a Chinese man. I called out to her and the Chinese man came and then carried Herbert to Miss Hartford's house, I carrying baby and Mildred and Evan waiting in the wood. I then went back and carried Evan to Miss Hartford's house, and was going back for Mildred, but met her on the way trying to walk. She could only walk a few steps and then I heard a cracking sound in her knee and she fell down.

Unsure about what to do, the children hid in the wood until they heard the sound of a horn calling the attackers to retreat. Finally, they saw two figures coming towards them. One was Flora Codrington who, despite a severe slash to her face, had survived the massacre by pretending to be dead. Accompanying her was a Chinese man, who immediately came over and picked up Herbert. Leaving Evan and Mildred for the moment in the wood but carrying the baby, Kathleen walked down the hill with them to the holiday cottage of an American missionary. She then went back to the wood and carried Evan to the house. Returning for a third time to help her sister, she found Mildred trying to walk and half-carried, half-dragged, her to join the others.

It was not long before a CMS missionary, Rev H. S. Phillips, appeared. Hearing the commotion from a distance, by the time he arrived at the scene of the attack, the houses were already burning and one of Roberts's Chinese translation assistants led him down to the survivors in the cottage. Phillips did his best to tend the children's and Flora's wounds. Mildred's right-knee joint had been speared to a depth of six inches. Herbert had suffered a crushing blow to his skull, and a deep four inch cut into his neck which was bleeding profusely. Evan had been severely beaten and stabbed in his left thigh. Baby Hilda's face was speared through the cheek, right eye, and forehead.[5]

It was not until twelve hours later that medical help arrived, and almost a whole day before transport to the hospital in Foochow was arranged. For the first leg of the journey, the children were carried through the night and following day in rickety sedan chairs over steep mountainous paths to the township of Cui-kau on the Min River. It was during this exhausting trek, while they were resting at a wayside inn, that Herbert finally passed

5. *Dublin Daily Express,* 16 September 1895, 5.

away. On being told about his death, Mildred cried: "How glad father and mother will be to see him."[6]

Throughout the entire journey, groups of local Chinese appeared expressing deep sympathy for the children. At Cui-kau, they were met by a relief party from the capital organised by the American Consul and the Anglican Archdeacon. As they boarded the launch:

> It was touching to see the little girls, though faint from want of food themselves, caring tenderly for their tiny brother, Evan, three and a half years old, throughout the rest of the journey. None of their clothing, except that which they wore, had been rescued. Evan was in his little night-things only, on that journey lasting from Thursday to Sunday, and Kathleen carried baby Hilda in her arms a great part of that time.[7]

The two-day voyage down the Min was profoundly sad. This was not only because of the injured children on board. Not far behind them a second boat was carrying small coffins containing the mutilated and charred bodies of their parents and nanny, as well as the Saunders sisters and other lady missionaries. After an overnight stop halfway to Foochow, the entourage boarded a small steamer for the final part of the journey.

Around midday on 4 August, they docked at the wharf on Nantai Island and were greeted by a solemn crowd waiting to hear the full extent of injuries from the massacre. The children and Flora were taken immediately to the CMS Hospital. It was all but impossible to prise the baby away from Kathleen until a female missionary nurse, in Chinese dress, was able to gently draw Hilda into her arms.

大屠殺中倖存的孩子們

The Stewarts back in Ireland first heard of the massacre two days after it happened. Arthur was staying with aunt Tem in Dublin, while Philip and James had gone on holiday to the Isle of Man with grandmother Smyly. On Arthur's return from sailing that day, he was met by his uncle George.

> I knew from his face that something distressing had happened. He went with me to Brighton Lodge and there told me that a wire had come to CMS to say that father and mother had been killed and two of the children; the other three all injured—Mildred

---

6. Barnes, *Beyond the Great Wall*, 147.
7. Barnes, *Beyond the Great Wall*, 148.

dangerously. The blow was too stunning for active sensation; but I do remember that, if I had ever really prayed in my life, I did so that night, and I know I prayed specifically that Mildred's life might be saved. I am certain that the intention began to form in my mind that I would give my life to God in China.[8]

The tragic news was then conveyed to Louisa's sister, Ellen Smyly, so she could pass the message on to the other boys. As soon as Ellen knew the full extent of the situation, she began planning a voyage to China to bring her nieces and nephew home.

In hospital, Mildred hovered between life and death for several days. The medical staff feared that, due to infection, they might need to amputate her injured leg. Evan, though not seriously hurt, was still in shock and remained deeply frightened by the whole experience. Kathleen, who showed such bravery and resilience during the journey, began to feel the weight of all that had occurred. As it happened, the children were being cared for in the Women's Wing of the hospital built through their mother's fund-raising efforts. The moving funeral, conducted by Archdeacon Wolfe, was held at 5am on 6 August in the European cemetery on Nantai Island. It was attended by most of the foreign residents and dignitaries in the city. According to a first-hand description:

> In the centre was a black draped box, smaller than a coffin, and on it the names of Robert and Louisa Stewart, and the words, "Lovely and pleasant in their lives, in their deaths they were not divided." The last part of the service was read around the large grave where, side by side, only separated from each other by a low brick partition rested those ten precious forms . . . There was a wealth of beautiful white wreaths to cover each coffin and each bore a text chosen by Mr Phillips.[9]

Four days later, on 10 August, little Hilda succumbed to her wounds and died. She was buried the next day alongside her parents. By now, "news of the horrific incident had ricocheted around the world. It was highlighted in major newspapers in the US, Australia, Britain, Ireland and China . . . Diplomatic briefings and updates were regularly made to the relevant Government agencies. Public 'indignation meetings' were held in places like Shanghai, Hong Kong and London. Prayers encircled the world from Canada to New Zealand."[10]

---

8. A. Stewart, *After Seventy Years*, 9.
9. Barnes, *Behind the Great Wall*, 149–150.
10. Banks & Banks, *Valley of the Shadow*, 20.

Graves of massacre victims

According to the former British Consul in Foochow, who had just returned to England after thirty years in China:

> I am quite certain that the massacres at Kucheng are not due to the people themselves. I knew both Mr and Mrs Stewart intimately. They were always exceptionally friendly with the Chinese, and had established the most cordial relationships years ago . . . In my opinion the outrages are partly due to the demonstration caused by the Japanese victories and by the absolute collapse of the Chinese Government. These massacres, which we deplore today, are probably caused by a dissatisfaction with the local authorities and the Central Government . . . I could understand some missionaries being attacked, but, as I said before, it is a mystery to me why Mr and Mrs Stewart should have been attacked, and it is quite clear that, in the first place, the murderers were strangers to the town, and that their object was an indirect one.[11]

On 13 August, a large public Memorial Service, organized by CMS, was held at Exeter Hall in the Strand, London, with representatives from CIM, London Missionary Society, Baptist and Methodist denominations. Llewelyn Lloyd and his wife, on furlough back in England, were also

---

11. This was Mr T. Waters in the *St James's Gazette*, 9 August 1895, 8.

present, as well as William Cassels, Bishop of West China. Henry Fox, the CMS Secretary, led the meeting. There was a solemn atmosphere, with many shedding tears.[12] In her annual Queen's Speech to the British Parliament on 15 August, Her Majesty Queen Victoria specifically mentioned the massacre in Hwasang. A copy of this was immediately telegraphed to newspapers in all British colonies.[13]

Commission of Inquiry in Foochow

The same day an official six-week Commission of Inquiry into the incident began in Foochow. Its distinguished members made special trips to investigate the site, took photographs, interviewed survivors, and gathered evidence from those first on the scene. At the same time, the Chinese military identified, hunted down, and arrested around one hundred suspects. These men became the focus of an internationally publicized trial in Foochow.

> As this unfolded, political pressures were brought to bear by both British and Chinese authorities. Both sides agreed that severe penalties were justified, but some of the British desired wider reparations, while some of the Chinese sought to restrict punishment to the leading perpetrators. Behind the scenes a compromise was finally reached. The most serious murderers,

12. Yueng, *Streams of Life*, 18.
13. *Home News for India, China and the Colonies*, 16 August, 1895.

26 in all, were beheaded and their bodies displayed at the entrance to the South Gate in Foochow as a warning to future terrorist acts. A further 19 were banished or imprisoned for life, 27 incarcerated for ten to fifteen years, and 20 for lesser periods.[14]

The Chinese government offered to pay the compensation to CMS for their losses, but CMS declined in favor of extending forgiveness. Peking's response was the making of an expensive memorial silk banner to commemorate the deaths of people they considered martyrs.

Two days after the trial started, Ellen boarded the *SS Campania* in Dublin, docking in New York. Travelling overland to the West Coast, she caught another ship across the Pacific. By the time the vessel reached Shanghai, a telegram arrived to say that Mildred was still unable to travel. After landing in Foochow, Ellen spent the next five weeks at the hospital, never far from the children's side.[15] She was able to attend some of the trial and see face to face those who had murdered her sister, brother-in-law, niece and nephew. Around the time of sentencing she was asked by a Chinese Christian couple who regularly visited the perpetrators whether the family would like to send them a message. Her reply was simply: "Tell them from me that we freely forgive them . . . the children have frequently said this to me. They feel no resentment. Their great desire is to be missionaries themselves."[16]

Within weeks Mildred's surgery and treatment restored her mobility, though left her with a permanent limp. Evan became a little more settled but mostly didn't talk very much. Kathleen largely regained her strength, yet continued to suffer vivid nightmares. When Ellen was finally able to make travel arrangements for Ireland, Mildred pleaded that they *must* stay because: "No one can be spared from the work now!"[17] For other reasons, leaving China was especially difficult for the girls. They were grieving not only their parents but others like Nelly and Topsy whom they had grown to love as older sisters. At least it was good to know that Flora was recovering well, and that they would see her again when she returned to the UK. All of them were looking forward to reuniting with their brothers and wider family.

For the sake of the children, Ellen decided that the longer route through the Suez Canal was preferable. This would also have the advantage of a doctor being available for the whole trip. It took them about six weeks to finally dock in Dublin. Though the family worked hard at shielding the

14. Banks & Banks, *Valley of the Shadow*, 21.
15. See Smyly, *Erin's Hope*, no page.
16. Barnes, *Beyond the Great Wall*, 151.
17. Barnes, *Beyond the Great Wall*, 141.

children, particularly the girls, from inquisitive reporters, their arrival inevitably generated strong interest. Kathleen's account of the massacre had already received wide coverage in local as well as major newspapers. It was more difficult to protect the children, even the older boys, from well-intentioned interest by churchgoers keen to express sympathy that could at times become overwhelming.

大屠殺中倖存的孩子們

The Stewart and Smyly families agreed that creating a stable environment was now the priority for the three younger children. Initially there was some debate about which side of the family should take day-to-day responsibility for this. Since the three older boys were already based with maiden aunt Tem, it was ultimately decided they should live with her in 'Brighton Lodge', Monkstown, where she had moved after her father's death at the end of 1891. The Smylys would contribute to the cost of employing additional servants and household expenses. Robert's brother, George, would continue as the children's legal guardian, and oversee the financial costs of their upbringing.

That first Christmas together was incredibly hard as the children thought back to happier times with their parents in Bedford just three years earlier. Arthur wrote that he felt like "a ship without a rudder. My life had revolved around father and mother and everything had been done with them in mind. Prizes were worth winning . . . in order to get a delighted letter from father or to see the delight in mother's face. Then the objective was taken away—why bother to work!"[18] For a time the older girls found themselves between two worlds. Mildred continued to struggle with her leg and sometimes felt socially isolated. At least the two of them knew they had each other to lean on during these early months.

At the beginning of 1896, the older boys returned to school at Haileybury, midway between London and Cambridge, in Hertfordshire. It was an independent Public School whose motto was 'Fear God and honour the King', and aim was to develop students' 'moral compass' and 'service to the Empire'. Arthur was now in Sixth Form, a Prefect and, in his own words, "happy and contented." Philip, two years behind, had joined the school's Cadets, which focussed on "leadership and teamwork," and was doing well in athletics. James, in Second Form, though sometimes vulnerable to sickness, was already excelling academically. In Dublin, Mildred was studying

---

18. A. Stewart, *After Seventy Years*, 9.

for the three-year Junior Certificate in a nearby Protestant Girls Secondary College, with Kathleen preparing to join her in a few month's time.

A regular feature of life in Brighton Lodge was family prayers at breakfast. Aunt Tem usually led these, but each of the children contributed their own special needs for the day and people they wanted to pray for. Following their mother's example, Mildred and Kathleen had already developed the habit of reading 'Daily Light', a short collection of bible passages grouped around a common theme, designed for use in the morning and evening. On Saturday afternoons they enjoyed going for walks in nearby People's Park or beside Scotsman's Bay, watching the ferries come into Dun Laoghaire harbour from Wales, or listening to the band playing on East Pier. On Sunday mornings the whole household attended Monkstown Parish Church, beginning with Sunday School for the children, followed by the Morning Service, often not getting back for lunch till 2pm. In the evenings they all gathered around aunt Tem at the piano and sang their favorite hymns, including ones their father had taught them.

All the Stewart children continued to maintain an interest in missionary work, especially in China. Each month their aunt received copies of *CMS Awake*, which sometimes contained stories and photos about what was happening in Fukien. Their hearts leapt when occasionally a letter came in the morning mail with a Chinese stamp because they knew it was from one of their Kucheng 'family'. One of these mentioned that money was being given by people from many countries to erect a statue of an angel with outstretched wings to be placed over the graves of the victims in Foochow. Sculpted out of fine Italian marble, this Martyrs' Memorial was to be dedicated on the anniversary of the massacre. CMS informed them that memorial services were also being arranged in major public venues and churches around the world.

When 1 August finally came, all six children were away on their annual holiday with members of both the Smyly and Stewart families. As they remembered the loss of their parents, brother, sister, and friends, the sadness was overwhelming. But the children took comfort from the fact that one day they would see them all again, and that their parents' sacrifice had led to a groundswell of those offering for missionary service in China.

Over the next few years life began to settle down for all the Stewart children. A focus on education helped them to gain some stability and direction. The eldest, Arthur, now almost nineteen, was thin and wiry, athletic and a keen cyclist. Though inordinately shy, he had a strong sense of responsibility. In Michaelmas term 1896, he went up to Trinity College, Cambridge University to study for a Bachelor of Arts in Theology. As he writes:

> What a wonderful place Cambridge seemed to be . . . so free from restriction. My first year I shared rooms in Malcolm Street with my cousin, Charlie Stewart . . . He was up quite frankly to play tennis and enjoy himself, and so he was not much help to me in getting a degree . . . The first to call on me were leaders of the CICCU [Cambridge Inter-Collegiate Christian Union] . . . and I was soon involved in the Christian life of the University . . . I frequently attended the daily prayer meeting, as well as the weekly meeting at Trinity College, and took my turn to lead and pray, though I suffered agonies in doing so, and thus I was being gradually trained.

As well as lectures in the Divinity School, he attended others at nearby Ridley Hall, the evangelical Anglican theological college, whose Principal had previously headed up the CMS Training College in Islington. A visit from the Travelling Secretary of the Student Volunteer Missionary Union [SVMU] had a life-changing impact upon Arthur.

> We had a long talk together and he asked me if I was willing to sign the SVMU Declaration that, if God showed the way, I would be willing to be a missionary. The idea had, of course, long been in my mind but never so definitely put, and I was not sure that I was ready for such a surrender. Finally, I said 'yes', and he gave me four lines which I repeated on my knees, then wrote on the fly-leaf of my bible:
>
> *I'll go where you want me to go, Lord,*
> *O'er mountains, o'er valley or sea.*
> *I'll do what you want me to do, Lord.*
> *I'll be what you want me to be.*
>
> Thus my surrender came about, and I was committed to the service of God, and I could never draw back. However, I still looked to the future with dread.[19]

After he finished at Haileybury, Philip decided to continue a Smyly family tradition of doing medicine at Trinity College in Dublin. This was also where his father had studied Law prior to his call to China. The College, dating back to the sixteenth century, was Ireland's equivalent of Cambridge or Oxford, and had strong connections with teaching hospitals in the city. In appearance Phil, as he was generally known, was more like his mother and, as a second child, more relaxed and sociable than his older brother. He began working towards a Bachelor in Medicine and Bachelor in Surgery. During his studies, Philip regularly attended chapel services. He also took

19. A. Stewart, *After Seventy Years*, 9–10 for this and the previous quote.

a particular interest in the DUFM, which his father had helped found, as it sent, prayed for and supported, Trinity College graduates as missionaries to Fukien province.

After Philip left, James had two more years at Hayleybury. Jim, as everyone called him, had his father's handsome looks and his mother's winsomeness. Although intellectually gifted—always wanting to think through issues—he got on really well with ordinary people. Unfortunately, during his last year at school he contracted pleurisy, which led to rheumatic fever, and finally an abscess on the lung which was diagnosed as tuberculosis. For months he was very ill, but was always buoyed by visits from Arthur, who cycled forty miles each way to and from Cambridge to visit him. After resting up in Monkstown during the summer vacation in 1899, he learned that despite his illness he too had gained entrance to Trinity College to study for an Arts degree. During his first year at university, perhaps because of the courses he was taking, perhaps because of his protracted illness, James began to have some serious doubts about the Christian faith. Though he continued to attend church on Sundays and chapel services during the week, inwardly he was struggling to work out what he really believed.

When Mildred completed her Junior Certificate in Dublin, she seems to have worked in the Smyly Homes and Schools. Its work in housing orphans and educating poor children had expanded over the years. Knowing that Mildred ultimately wanted to return to China, her aunt Ellen, who now headed up the work, felt that serving as a volunteer teacher would be valuable missionary preparation. During this time, Kathleen continued to do well at school and Evan was taught by a governess at home.

In the first half of 1900, the Stewarts began to hear news about violent protests against Western influence in northern China. The main instigators were members of what became known as the Boxer Movement, which opposed the way foreign influence was eroding traditional Chinese lifestyle, culture and religion. Christianity increasingly became a target, especially in remote areas where people were more superstitious and official protection was weaker. In late May, reports came in from various provinces of groups surrounding mission stations, dragging out their occupants, killing some on the spot, and taking others to temples to be tortured. As well, thousands of Chinese converts were set alight, hacked to death, or skinned alive.[20] In July, after Empress Cixi issued an edict that endorsed the uprising, masses of Boxers, supported by elements in the Chinese army, besieged more than a thousand Westerners—including missionaries and their families, and three thousand Chinese Christians—in the foreign legations at Peking.

---

20. Banks and Banks, *Faraway Pagoda*, 47–48.

Kathleen and Mildred at Brighton Lodge

This turmoil immediately took Mildred and Kathleen back to their horrific experience in Hwasang. When they saw newspaper photos of some of their missionary friends in Fukien who were considered to be in peril, the girls were distressed and urged everyone they knew to pray for them. They were relieved when, in mid-August, an international peace-keeping force finally reached Peking, dispersed the attackers, and rescued those who were besieged. The Empress's reluctant decision to reverse her support for the Boxers led to a quietening of the situation in the rest of the country.

The arrival of the new century on 1 January 1901 was signalled by celebrations throughout the United Kingdom. These were more muted in Ireland, partly because of underlying resentment of many against British rule, and partly because the Irish economy was in such a poor state. Its population had fallen by a quarter of million in a decade. Most people lived in small farmsteads and grimy urban tenements. With no old age pensions or social welfare arrangements, the only place of refuge for the aged, infirm and unemployed was the workhouse. In Dublin, nearly a quarter of all children died before their first birthday, a third of all deaths resulted from chest infections, and life expectancy was less than anywhere else in the UK. In response, nationalism was on the rise. The anti-British Daughters of Erin was founded, and other political and cultural organisations joined forces that later became Sinn Féin. To counter this, the Chief Secretary implemented policies of the British Conservative government to reduce support for independence. The only area of life experiencing progress was the revival in Irish language, literature, and culture.[21] Uncle George, and others in the Stewart and Smyly family circles, were in favor of a compromise position where the Irish administered 'Home Rule' under the authority of the British Parliament.[22] A few weeks later, the unexpected death of Queen Victoria after a reign of nearly sixty-five years, was deeply felt around the British Commonwealth. For the Stewart children, this loss was compounded by the death in May of their beloved grandmother Ellyn Smyly.

大屠殺中倖存的孩子們

The next few years marked a new stage in the lives of all the children. Arthur had graduated from Cambridge the year before, a time in which, he wrote, God was "becoming more real to me."[23] Encouraged by his involvement in children's beach missions and evangelistic boys camps during vacations, he now felt ready to offer as a candidate to CMS. Its committee advised him to take a six-months medical course at Livingstone College, named after the famous missionary, in London. "One difference it made to me was to reduce my fear of ordination. I began to feel that God was really calling me to a serious task." Ordained a deacon in 1901, and priest the following year, he began a curacy at St. Paul's Church, Canonbury, a poorer suburb in north London.

> Only a few weeks later, after I had settled in, [the Vicar] was offered the living of Holy Trinity, Cambridge. He asked me to go with him; I wanted to return to the friendly and comfortable life of Cambridge, but I knew I had been directed to stay at Canonbury. But what a prospect! . . . Ordained only two months I was alone in a parish of over ten thousand people . . . It was like throwing a non-swimmer into deep water. I had a slight breakdown in health . . .[24]

21. For further reading on this, see Mulhall, *New Day Dawning*.
22. Jackson, *Home Rule*.
23. A. Stewart, After Seventy Years, 10.
24. A. Stewart, After Seventy Years, 11.

Fortunately, it was not long before a new Vicar arrived.

In 1901, Philip had almost completed his Bachelor of Medicine and Bachelor of Surgery at Trinity College. Like his maternal uncle, Sir William Josiah Smyly, he decided to specialise in gynaecology and began a Bachelor's in Obstetrics, a program that was unique to medical studies in Ireland. He regularly attended Christian student meetings in the College and made friends there. The final two years of his program focussed on clinical experience in a university teaching hospital. During this time, his interest in the military, another family tradition, reasserted itself, and he began to think about serving in the Royal Army Medical Corps [RAMC]. This was a specialist non-combatant group in the British Army that provided medical services to all personnel and their families in both war and peace.

At the start of term in January 1901, James's health continued to be precarious, and medical advice was to move to a warmer, drier climate. He remembered that, despite his father's taxing schedule in Australia, Robert's health had greatly improved during his stay there. His plan was to complete his Bachelor of Arts at the University of Sydney. Having resolved many of the doubts about his faith, he was now wanting to pursue theological studies with a view to ultimately working in China. So, James wrote to Archbishop Suamarez Smith, who had sponsored his father's visit to Australia in 1892, about doing this at Moore Theological College on the edge of the university's campus.

On receiving a positive response, he sailed to Sydney and in the second half of the year began studying at the university. Shortly after his arrival, James was invited to assist at a major CMS Exhibition, highlighting fields where missionaries from Australia were working. The China and Japan section was organized by Amy Oxley, on furlough from Foochow. She had known Robert Stewart during his Australian visit, and was initially going to join James's parents in Kucheng, a plan which was interrupted by their deaths.[25] In 1902, he was elected President of the university's Christian Union. He also attended St Matthias' Church in Paddington, and taught in its Sunday School.

After completing his BA, with second class honours in Greek and Philosophy, James studied at Moore Theological College with Principal Nathaniel Jones in preparation for the Oxford and Cambridge Preliminary, gaining First Class results. His faith was deepened by Jones's blend of thoughtful evangelicalism, compassionate social concern, and Keswick-style spirituality.[26] In

---

25. For a full account of Amy's life and work see our book '*They Shall See His Face*'.

26. On Principal Nathaniel Jones' theological, social and spiritual convictions see the excellent study by John A. MacIntosh, *Anglican Evangelicalism*, 81–121.

March 1903, Dr John R. Mott, founder of the Student Volunteer Movement [SVM] and President of the World Student Christian Federation, made a second visit to Australia.[27] As James had now become Australian Secretary of the SVM, he was asked by Mott to accompany him on a speaking tour of all the university campuses in the country. During this trip James discussed with Mott his future in China, in particular the strategic nature of Christian work among university students. Helped by the Australian climate his health steadily improved, and by the time he returned to England at the end of the year, it was fully restored. James then applied to the Bishop of Winchester about serving in his Diocese. In mid-1904 he was ordained and appointed to St James Church, Shirley, on the edge of Southampton.

James (3rd from left, back row) at Moore College

After finishing her Junior Certificate, and training as a 'pupil teacher', Kathleen was encouraged to 'complete' her education at a finishing school in the historic Belgian city of Bruges. This beautiful location, with its canals and cobble-stone squares, had become one of the world's finest tourist destinations, attracting wealthy British and French visitors. This female boarding school was primarily designed to prepare well-to-do students for marriage by training them in French language and culture, household management, etiquette, and grooming. Always gregarious, Kathleen adapted well to this

---

27. Mott's visits to Australia are discussed in Stuart Piggin and Robert D. Linder, *Fountain of Public Prosperity*, 499–501,

opportunity to meet people from other parts of Europe and to experience a larger world. On Kathleen's return from Bruges, Arthur wrote:

> After two years in the Parish, my health began to flag. Then uncle George suggested that I should rent a small house and ask Kathleen to run it for me. It was a wonderful suggestion, for it met her need too; she has finished her education and was fretting for something to do. We rented a small house in Canonbury Park and there followed two happy years, Kathleen winning her way into the affections of the people. As well as teaching Sunday-school and helping with the YWCA, she gave missionary addresses in other parishes, occasionally with amusing results. On one occasion she asked the superintendent where she was to go, and his reply was, 'What class are you in dear?' And Kathleen had to explain that she was *not* a school-girl but the speaker![28]

According to Arthur, her happiest work was in a club for undisciplined and recalcitrant factory girls, where she ended up making some lifelong friends.

Mildred especially missed James, who was closest to her in age, while he was away in Australia. At the Smyly Schools and Homes she was now not only teaching but increasingly drawn into assisting her aunts in making decisions about the future of the institution. Though sometimes in pain from her disability, she learnt to get on with the work she believed God had called her to do.

After a time at Preparatory school in Dublin, Evan enrolled at Wellington College in Berkshire. Because of its historic link with the Duke who had defeated Napoleon at Waterloo, and its distinguished reputation for sport, uncle George thought it was a good fit for someone who had both military and athletic interests. In the spring of 1904, Evan moved from Dublin and began boarding there.

The following year was a decisive one for the Stewart family. Arthur, assisted by Kathleen, had now been working in the parish at Canonbury for two years. Earlier discussions with CMS had focussed on his going to the province where Robert and Louisa had served. For a couple of years, Arthur had been in regular correspondence with Bishop Joseph Hoare in Hong Kong, whose Diocese included Fukien. During a brief visit by the Bishop to England, the two met and talked about this. The Bishop sympathised with Arthur's desire to follow in his father's footsteps but pointed out that other missionaries were now continuing Robert and Louisa's work. He felt that Hong Kong was the place where similar challenges existed. Hoare suggested

---

28. A. Stewart, After Seventy Years, 12.

that Arthur join Rev G. A. Bunbury, Principal of the small Theological College that was training Chinese catechists for congregations in all four provinces of south China. Hearing of Kathleen's desire to return to China, even though she was not yet a CMS candidate, the Bishop offered to organise a teaching position for her on the staff of the Diocesan Girls' School.

Arthur as a Curate in London

Arthur and Kathleen felt that this arrangement was God's way of getting both of them back to China together. They were also very aware that this was taking place just after the tenth anniversary of their parents' death. As Arthur wrote: "All this came at the last minute, and at the Farewell Meeting in Exeter Hall my name was still on the list for Fukien. In October we sailed in SS *Palawan* . . . we reached Hong Kong on December 11 and what a thrill I felt! I was to start my life work."[29]

---

29. A. Stewart, After Seventy Years, 13

3

Unfinished Business in China (1905–1914)

As they sailed past the scattered islands surrounding Hong Kong, its magnificent Victoria Harbour framed by towering mountains opened up before them. Though their memories were hazy, both of them had stayed briefly in the city as children. Arthur thought he could remember the site of St Paul's College on the island where he and Philip had spent a few days in 1892 en route to Ireland. Kathleen was able to point out the path of the cable-tram up to the Peak which she had glimpsed in 1895. On the opposite side of the *SS Palawan* they saw a range of hills beyond Kowloon, which marked the limit of the New Territories ceded by China to the British colony a few years earlier.

When the ship docked, the newcomers were greeted at the wharf by Archdeacon William Banister and his wife Mary, in whose home they were initially staying. They felt this was a gift from God, as the Banisters had been good friends of their parents. Kathleen recalled their kindness to her in Foochow before aunt Ellen arrived to take them back to Ireland. There was much to talk about, not only about the past but also life in Hong Kong as well as their future work.

Within a few days, they met up with Bishop Joseph Hoare and his wife, Ellen (nee Gough). She had been an Irish CEZMS missionary who, along with Louisa, worked with Mrs Ahok in Foochow. The Bishop confirmed that the Stewarts' first step was to learn the language. Though both remembered a little Fukienese from their childhood, they now had to study Cantonese, the form of Chinese mostly spoken in south-east China. This would occupy most of the next year, since only after passing a formal examination could they take up their teaching positions.

Victoria Harbour, Hong Kong, early 1900s

In early 1906, the Chinese New Year holidays provided an opportunity to begin exploring the Colony. The population of Hong Kong at the time was around half a million, mostly Chinese with a few thousand Westerners. The eastern section of the city housed British shops, hotels, post offices, and libraries, as well as military barracks, parade grounds, and sports fields. The western section was filled with Chinese shops, warehouses, markets, apothecaries, and tea houses. The city had already been electrified, and the first automobiles were beginning to appear among the mass of rickshaws and sedan chairs. Transport across the harbor was by ferry and sampans. Arthur and Kathleen were surprised just how 'British' life was for most non-Chinese, how much foreigners mixed predominantly in their own circles, and how few of them spoke the language fluently. Apart from servants working in expat homes, and some well-educated Chinese in business and finance, life was largely segregated. They were disappointed to learn that while a small Chinese elite acted as mediators between the government and populace, the latter had virtually no say in political decisions.[1]

While continuing to learn the language, the Stewarts could only contribute to the Mission in limited ways. Arthur was occasionally able to

---

1. A helpful account of Hong Kong's development in this period is provided by Carroll, *History of Hong Kong*, 61–88.

preach at an occasional English service at the Cathedral and share the gospel at CMS gatherings for British soldiers and sailors. As instruction was only in English, Kathleen was initially able to assist in the recently established St Stephen's Girls College. Just after the mid-year summer break, however, a terrible calamity struck Hong Kong.

The city's Observatory gave less than a thirty-minute warning of a typhoon that hit the Colony just after 9 o'clock on 18 September. The impact was devastating, especially on the many fishing villages along the coast and nearby islands. Among the few non-Chinese seriously affected was Bishop Hoare.

> The Bishop was on a preaching tour embracing the villages along the coast in the direction of Castle Peak and Capsuimoon. It was his ... custom on these tours to live on his houseboat, and he was on board with four Chinese converts when the typhoon burst. With the Bishop assisting at the tiller, great efforts were apparently made to run for shelter, but the wind was so violent and the sea so heavy that no craft of that description could hope to live in it. The Bishop, who was reputed to be a strong swimmer, stripped himself to his singlet, as his companions had done, and knelt down in prayer. Just after this the boat was capsized and broken up by the heavy seas ... The Bishop was last seen in the water clinging to some of the wreckage. Search for the body was made for several days but without success. [2]

The typhoon caused severe damage to streets and wharves as well as extensive disruption of day-to-day life. Destruction of property amounted to over a million pounds and, most tragically, several thousand residents were killed.

It was a stressful few hours for Mrs Hoare before conclusive news of her husband's drowning finally reached her. Kathleen, who had been invited as a companion at the Bishop's House while he was traveling, was able to offer comfort at such a terrible time. The news came to Arthur as a huge shock, the more so when the Principal of the theological college decided to transfer it to Canton, ninety miles away up the Pearl River. These two blows left him feeling that "the reason for my coming to Hong Kong was taken away ... I remained in Hong Kong at a loose end. What was I to do? Had a mistake been made? Patience has never been my strong point. How often I

---

2. 'Calamatous Typhoon', University of Hong Kong. This information was brought by two of the crew who managed to hold on to some of the wreckage and were eventually cast ashore.

have had to quote to myself, "O rest in the Lord. Wait patiently for him." I had no definite objective before me."[3]

Arthur threw himself into completing language study. By the end of the year, he passed his first examination and was asked by the theological college Principal if he could join him in Canton immediately. Though this meant leaving Kathleen in Hong Kong, CMS had now approved her as a probationer missionary, with a maintenance allowance and accommodation, while she taught at the Diocesan Girls School.

At the end of June 1907, Gerard Lander was consecrated Bishop of Victoria at St John's Cathedral. Like Arthur, he was a graduate of Trinity College and Ridley Hall in Cambridge. Since the summer holidays had already begun, he and Kathleen were able to attend the ceremony together. The Bishop's first wife had died in England five years before, leaving two daughters, Kitty, aged twelve, and Dorothy, eleven. After his remarriage, his wife Margaret was expecting their first child. [4]

Towards the end of the summer, Arthur received an invitation to join the staff of St Stephen's College as a half-time teacher. This school, whose headmaster was an Australian, Rev E. Judd Barnett, was set up by CMS for the sons of well-to-do Chinese. Its staff included both English and Chinese masters, and had an enrolment of 150 students. Arthur's first experience of teaching school students gave him a new interest. He saw at first hand the importance of Christian education that prepared young men for every profession, not just ministry in the church.

By now, Kathleen's language skills had improved to the point where she could teach in Cantonese. Her warmth and enthusiasm led to a number of the girls becoming life-long friends.[5] Through these friendships, she was able to initiate home visits to their mothers, the first missionary in the city to do this, which led to some women coming to faith. Along with her work at the Diocesan Girls School, she also taught Scripture at the Anglo-Chinese Preparatory School attended by the younger sons and daughters of wealthy Chinese.

One day during this time, Arthur records:

> "I chanced to be in a photographer's shop and there was served by a nice-looking young fellow who later began coming to see me for instruction for baptism . . . by the name of Thomas Chan.

---

3. A. Stewart, *After Seventy Years*, 11, with the scripture quotation coming from Psalm 37:7 (KJV).

4. More detail on the Lander's arrival is in Wolfendale, *History of St John's Cathedral*, 111.

5. *The Chimes*, 36.2, 1947, 6–7.

In various conversations with Chinese Christians, they pointed out the need for a school, similar to St Stephen's but with lower fees. Thomas Chan once told me that his great desire was to teach. 'Then', said I, 'let us start a school together.'"[6]

Later that year Bishop Lander invited CMS to recommence the Anglo-Chinese Boys School—which during previous decades had started and stopped several times—in the premises vacated by the theological college.[7] They agreed to this initiative and asked Arthur to begin planning for it, which he did with the help of Thomas Chan.

In the mid-year vacation of 1908, Arthur and Kathleen had their first opportunity to travel to Foochow where they had been born. They decided to attend the annual Missionary Conference held at Kuliang (now Guliang) in the mountains above the city. Here they met up with missionaries who had known their parents and shared with them the ongoing impact of their work. After the Conference they spent some time exploring the Wu-Shi-shan area, site of the Stewarts' first house and school, as well as Nantai Island, where Robert's theological college and Louisa's Bible-women's school were flourishing. The most moving part of their visit was placing flowers on the graves of their parents, brother, and sister, who had died in Hwasang. They felt Robert and Louisa would be pleased that two, and soon four, of their children were back serving God in China.

For the past three years, James and Mildred had been on their journeys toward China. Before starting in the parish of Shirley, James talked with Arthur and Kathleen about their experience of working together, and decided to invite Mildred to join him in Southampton. It was a growing parish with a church that could seat up to a thousand. This gave them both experience in a range of ministries in preparation for China. After three years in the parish, James applied to CMS, was accepted, and in early 1907 moved to London to start a year's training at its college in Islington.

Mildred also approached CMS, but was told that, since her permanent limp could be an impediment on the mission field, she could only be granted provisional acceptance. A final decision would depend on a medical assessment after time at the 'The Willows', or Mildmay Home, the CMS ladies training center in London. Alongside biblical studies and theology, as well as the history, geography, and religion of China, this provided practical experience of working among the poor in the East End. Students led mothers groups, cottage meetings, ministry to factory girls, and house-to-house

---

6. A. Stewart, After Seventy Years, 13.

7. The history and influence of mission-based schools in Hong Kong to this time is discussed in Leung, Impact of Mission Schools.

visitation.[8] At the end of this year-long training, to strengthen her application Mildred decided to join a few other candidates in doing some basic nursing at nearby Bethnal Green Hospital. Fortunately, after several medical examinations, she was classified fit for service and appointed to the same region as her brother in West China.

Mildred before going to China

James had set out for China in March 1908, staying a few days en route with Arthur and Kathleen in Hong Kong. As it was more than three years since they had seen each other, this reunion meant a lot to all of them, and they celebrated together the return of the third Stewart to China. The visit also helped James begin to reacquaint himself with Chinese culture. He provides a graphic account of the following 850-miles overland journey to Szechwan (now Sichuan).

> The long journey from the coast was full of interest, and the crowd of new impressions quite bewildering. That which stood out above all others was the sense of vastness. As we journeyed

---

8. See further Welch. 'The Willows', Appendix, and, more generally, Cheeseman, Training for Service, 65–77.

on, day after day, and week after week, passing lonely hamlets, villages, and great walled cities, black with age, we received gradually a conception of the immensity of this land, such as no figures could convey. The cities themselves were full of interest—the narrow, crowded streets and open shops, the strange odours that met one at every town, the mangey dogs, street hawkers, crowded tea-shops, men carrying portable kitchens, water carriers, street barbers, etc., all mingling in one crowded, streaming mass of humanity, jostling and shouting as they went. The temples, too, with their hideous figures and dread representations of the horrors of hell, the wayside shrines in countless numbers, with incense-sticks burning before them, all gave one a deep sense of that power, only less than infinite, which holds these people down and ever seeks to drag them lower. The first experiences of Chinese inns are not easily forgotten. The dirt and the smells which can almost be cut, the pigs and insects innumerable. These, however, are details which one soon gets used to, and, after a little experience, almost ignores.[9]

While he was beginning language study, James was based in Teh-yang, with Rev Howard Taylor, in a mountainous area north-east of Chengtu (now Chengdu), the cultural center of Szechwan. In August, Howard took him on a lengthy horseback tour of remote areas in the province.[10] This introduced Jim to some of the distinctive ethnic cultures and exotic wildlife in the region that borders Tibet. The return journey led over a pass 14,000 feet above sea level, and he was fascinated to see the friendliness of the tribes-people and the size of crowds that gathered to hear Taylor preach the gospel. At the end of 1908, still grappling with learning Mandarin, James wrote:

> The first six months of a missionary's life is perhaps his worst, for he has not yet got his roots down into the new soil, and his helplessness in the language cuts him off from active work—the great cure for loneliness. Nevertheless, looking back over them, I feel more thankful than ever to God for having sent me to this land.[11]

---

9. J. R. Stewart, Annual Letters, 1907–1908, 28 November 1908.

10. The earlier history of the CMS mission in Szechwan is summarized in the classic survey by Stock, *Church Missionary Society*, 325–328.

11. J. R. Stewart, Annual Letters, 1907–1908, 28 November 1908.

大屠殺中倖存的孩子們

Two significant developments took place for Arthur in early 1909. On 5 February, the Anglo-Chinese Boys School in St Paul's College [SPC] opened. "Sixteen boys enrolled on that morning . . . At the end of the first year the school enrolment was fifty and the Chapel, which held forty, was overflowing."[12] It offered subjects studied for the English University entrance exams together with a traditional Chinese curriculum, an overtly Christian world-view and culture, and a fee structure that made it available to more than just wealthy families. Arthur chose as the College motto: "the fear of the Lord is the beginning of wisdom" (Proverbs 1:7 KJV), whose Hebrew original is best translated "The most important part of knowledge is reverence of the Lord".

At the same time, Arthur started a Chinese church in the College premises. Under his leadership as Vicar:

> . . . a small but enthusiastic group of Chinese Christians scattered throughout the eastern part of the city . . . used to meet on Sundays in the small chapel in the basement of the Bishop's House. Many of these 'catacomb Christians' came from beyond Happy Valley, facing a two-hour walk to attend service and never missing. This congregation extended rapidly . . . and outgrew the church. Then services were held out-of-doors on what was then the Bishop's tennis court; in rainy weather the verandah was used.[13]

As well as this Chinese-speaking church, there was an evening service in English. Here:

> Arthur Stewart was at his best. His fluent, eloquent sermons in simple English words which all could follow, were the subject of keen discussion afterwards by students in every University Hostel. The handsome young Irishman with the graceful pulpit manner, the musical voice, the remarkable eyes and the amazing fluency of speech must be well remembered and loved by hundreds of men and women who heard him in those days.[14]

By the end of 1910, enrolments had reached one hundred and fifty and doubled the following year, with a consequent increase in staff. This resulted in planning an extension and addition to the existing premises. This led to

---

12. A. Stewart, After Seventy Years, 13–14.
13. From the article 'A. D. Stewart', Wayfarer, 47.
14. 'A. D. Stewart', Wayfarer, 47–48.

the construction of a two storey building, with the school on the lower floor and a chapel above it used by the church on Sundays. Under the leadership of two well-known Hong Kong citizens, Dr Tso Seen Wan and Sir Kai Ho, the necessary funds soon came in, mainly through a generous donation by Dr Wu Ting Fang, an earlier graduate of the College, whose name was ascribed to the new Hall.[15] The Stewart family contributed a five panel stained-glass east window, with accompanying wall plaque, in memory of their parents.

Kathleen with Bishop and Mrs Lander

After more than six busy years in Hong Kong, the Stewarts were due to take their first furlough. In preparing to go back to 'Brighton Lodge', both took time to reflect on all that had happened since their arrival in the Colony. Arthur believed he now had a clearer grasp of God's purpose for his life, and Kathleen a developing sense of her future educational ministry. After

---

15. Fung, *From Devotion to Plurality*, 60. Dr Wu rose to national prominence in the Sun Yat-sen Government after the 1911 Revolution.

completion of the new building, and a public celebration of its opening in September 1911,[16] the two set off for Ireland.

James had now moved to Chengtu to help establish the first University in the whole of inland China. Six mission societies were involved—American Baptists and Episcopal Methodists, the United Church of Canada and Canadian Methodists, the Quakers and CMS from Great Britain and Ireland.[17] Six acres across the river from the city had been purchased, and each mission society had a section on which they were building student accommodation, a chapel, and staff residences, around a central administrative and teaching area. Along with another CMS missionary, a friend of Arthur's student days in Cambridge, James was to be Warden of the CMS student hostel and chapel. The University's aim was to establish faculties of Arts, Science, Medicine, Law, Engineering, and Agriculture, so that it would be unnecessary for any student in the Western provinces to go abroad for any course needed to equip them for any phase of life in China. All teaching would be in Chinese, and take place in a Christian atmosphere. Although preference would be given to suitable Christian applicants, the University was open to students of any religious persuasion or none. Instruction was due to begin in the second half of the year.[18]

Since Chengtu was the cultural capital of Szechwan, with strong links to Shanghai and Peking, it was the ideal place for this initiative. Often referred to as 'Little Peking', the city was designed around a vice-regal palace, its version of the Forbidden City. Encircled by massive city walls, it was entered through an impressive East Gate, and a broad paved thoroughfare, bounded by trees and laced with canals. Dozens of traditional buildings reflected the architecture of different periods in Chinese history, among which signs of modern influence were now making their appearance.[19] Individual buildings in the University itself exhibited a mixture of architectural styles.

Mildred was pleased to be joining James in Szechwan, not just because they would be working near one another, but because this was where the most pioneering CMS work was now taking place. As a family member wrote many years later: it was "all the more wonderful that [she] bravely went out to the wildest part of China when she ... could remember clearly all the terrors of her childhood. Wonderful isn't it, the power and courage God gave, I never knew her to show any sign of fear, whether she felt it or

16. The occasion was reported in *The Hong Kong Telegraph*, 30 September 1911, 1.

17. On the role of the Mission more generally, see Boreham, "C.M.S. in the Union University", 25–30.

18. On the development of this institution, see the accounts by both Walmsley, *West China Union University*, and Taylor, *History of West China*.

19. This description is drawn from Banks & Banks, *Valley of the Shadow*, 32.

not . . .".[20] In parts of the province, bandit hold-ups and raids were common, and soldiers often broke the law instead of keeping the peace. In many respects, it was the 'Wild West' of China.

West China University Administration Building

Mildred left for Szechwan in early 1910. Since the journey took her through Hong Kong, she took the opportunity to stay for a while with her brother and sister at St Paul's College.[21] Excited by the presence of a fourth Stewart serving God in China, Kathleen relished this time with her older sister. Knowing that she would be involved in educational work, Mildred was pleased to visit the schools where Kathleen taught and visit the site where St Paul's College would be located.

On reaching Szechwan in May, she remembered her plea to aunt Ellen on leaving Foochow fifteen years earlier about the need for young women to carry on the work in China. This desire was now a reality. On arrival in Mienchow (now Mianyang), headquarters of the CMS Mission, she was warmly greeted by fellow missionaries "both for her father's and her brother's sake."[22] They immediately sent word to James, who was two-and-a-half days travel away in Chengtu.

It was in the smaller nearby center of Mienchuh that Mildred began her first year of Mandarin study. This city was on the edge of a region considered one of the great food-bowls of China. Its fertile soil and temperate

20. Letter from R. C. Taylor, 30 July 1959, courtesy of his grandson, David Taylor.

21. Her visit is noted in Bishop Ingham's Diary, *CMS Home Gazette*, April, 1910, 9 during his visit to the Colony.

22. Western China Original Papers, 1909–1910, no page number.

climate made it possible to grow crops like sugar cane, peanuts, cotton, tea, spices, tobacco—and unfortunately opium—all year around. The whole area, partly framed by high mountains, was however vulnerable to attack by roaming groups of bandits.

After the summer break, Mildred continued her language study at the CMS Ladies' House in Mienchow. In October, Rev Reginald Taylor, brother of Howard Taylor in Teh-yang, joined the CMS Mission. He and Mildred had a lot in common. Reg, as he was called, was a graduate of Cambridge University and Ridley Hall. After ordination, he served at a church in Sheffield before training with CMS in Islington. The following April, an Australian missionary arrived in Mienchow to begin language study. Mildred soon discovered that Victoria Mannett's decision to go to China was deeply influenced by reading about the massacre at Hwasang. This formed a bond between the two young women, and Mildred looked forward to introducing Victoria to James at the Mission's upcoming Annual Conference.

The Conference was scarcely over when reports of serious unrest in Chengtu began to surface. In the province, resentment had been building against the long-entrenched Qing Dynasty for some time. An underground League, comprised of a wide range of citizens, was beginning to organize open resistance against the Chinese Government and its local Viceroy. This group was primarily an anti-political, not anti-Christian, movement committed to modernizing the province. This was part of a larger campaign for national reform by leaders like Sun Yat-sen which became a catalyst for like-minded movements in other provinces.

When unrest emerged in Chengtu, the leaders of the League distributed leaflets indicating that no harm was intended towards missionaries. Their anger was chiefly directed at the Qing Dynasty's tardiness in modernizing the country, and its continuing refusal to share power with provincial governments. In August, several leading members of the League were arrested, and shots were fired at a number of peaceful demonstrators. In response, the League decided to stage an open rebellion.

Though the mission societies working in the province felt quite safe, the Chinese Viceroy and Consul-General advised their members to gather in cities close to a river so that, if needed, they could evacuate to its capital, Chungking (now Chongqing). Mildred had recently begun working with two other staff at a small mission station in Chung-pa, a day's journey from Mienchow. Because bandit activity had caused "great unrest" in the district, it took her and a female colleague a week to reach the CMS base safely.[23]

---

23. For more detail see the *Bulletin of the Diocese*, September 1911.

Unfinished Business in China (1905–1914) 59

In case there was an evacuation, James sent a message to Mildred suggesting she wait until he could join her. Since there might be a danger of pirates on the journey to Chungking, it would be safer to travel together. He also wrote to Victoria in Mienchow about what was happening. When, in Chengtu, the Vice-Consul ordered all missionaries to gather in the Canadian mission compound for safety, James laid low in his house and "slipped out of the city at daybreak" just before its gates were barred.[24] Avoiding unruly soldiers and aggressive bandits on the road took considerable courage. Since Mienchow itself was now on a war-footing, Mildred was relieved when just over two days later James arrived.

Soon they heard that the uprising was beginning to spread elsewhere. Outside Chengtu, several other cities were joining the rebellion. Most postal and telegraph services had shut down. When the Viceroy called in additional soldiers from other cities to quell the unrest, most of the Army switched its allegiance to the League. Their units then started to attack cities and towns in remote areas. One after another these capitulated, and prisoners in jails willing to join in the struggle were released.[25]

At the end of October, orders finally came from the Consul-General that all missionaries in the province must leave by river for the capital immediately. Jim, Mil, and Victoria joined a convoy of boats with around a hundred men, women, and children, for Chungking. Little did the evacuees know how long a trip lay before them. When they arrived in the capital, that city was also experiencing armed conflict, they had to sail hundreds of miles further along the Yangtze. The boats had to negotiate a way through the narrow channels, rapids, and whirlpools of the Three Gorges, so encircled by steep cliffs that daytime dimmed into twilight. Traveling through neighboring provinces, the missionaries saw at first-hand how quickly rebellion against the Qing Dynasty was escalating. En route they were challenged several times by revolutionary groups, once forced ashore to prove their credentials, but were then allowed to pass.

At Ichang, the next major river port several hundred miles downriver, there was again nowhere satisfactory to stay. This was severely disappointing as the missionaries had hoped to stay at the extensive CIM mission station there. The most dramatic moment in the trip occurred as the boats sailed further upriver, and were fired upon by soldiers on the shore who took

24. *Church Missionary Review*, February 1912, 107.

25. This description is partly drawn from Victoria Mannett's report in the *Hamilton Spectator*, 17 February 1912, and partly from the account of unrest in West China in the *Church Missionary Review*, February 1912, 106–108. A broader discussion of Szechwan's seminal role in the National Revolution is provided by Hsu, *Modern China*, 465–474.

them for enemies. Fortunately, no one on board was hurt. At Hankow, 'little Shanghai' as it was known, their next stopping-point, the evacuees hoped to join other missionaries from South China for whom it had become a place of refuge. When they arrived, however, revolutionary and government soldiers were fighting for control of the city. During an armistice between the combatants, the missionaries were alerted, had to transfer to a steamer, and head to the safety of the International Settlement in Shanghai. James and Mildred were relieved to arrive there in mid-December after a six-week journey of over 1800 miles.[26]

大屠殺中倖存的孩子們

The same year Arthur and Kathleen left for China, Evan began at Wellington College. Settling into boarding school in England was not easy for a boy who had spent his early years in Ireland. The first term was difficult as he struggled with the lack of privacy and homesickness, especially when he saw fellow boarders in his 'digs' at Blucher House receiving letters from their mothers. This experience led him to keep a photo of Louisa in his wallet, which he continued to do for the rest of his life. Although sometimes teased because of his tendency to stutter, this was offset by his ability in athletics, on one occasion winning the English Public Schools one hundred yards sprint competition. According to Wellington school magazines and Year Books, "Evan played rugby for his dormitory, and took part in swimming races, and a violin quartet."[27] He did well academically, especially in mathematics and history. Joining Wellington's Cadet Corps, with its mix of military discipline, field exercises, and survival skills, suited him well. The responsibility of being a Prefect also increased his confidence and capacity for leadership.

Returning to aunt Tem's in the holidays was always a welcome break, especially when Philip was able to get leave from his base and come home. He was initially stationed in Cork, only a few hours away, before being transferred in early 1908 to the Malta Garrison in the Mediterranean. For Evan, hearing stories about army life, historic sites in Malta, and travel to other parts of Europe, was always interesting. In the middle of 1910, he matriculated from Wellington College and began preparing for an Arts degree at TCD. During that summer, King George V and Queen Mary visited

---

26. The fullest account of this journey, by a CIM missionary evacuee, may be found in Service, *China Memoir*.

27. Courtesy of Caroline Jones, Archivist at Wellington College.

Dublin during their coronation tour, entering and leaving via Kingstown Harbour not far from Monkstown.

Evan (behind Master) at Blucher House

When Arthur and Kathleen returned from furlough in October, it only seemed like yesterday that they had lived at Brighton Lodge. Not having seen Evan for six and a half years, they found him "now grown up, a young man of nineteen . . . [and] had to begin all over again to know him."[28] Leisurely walks along the seafront, visits to favorite places in Dublin, and conversations after dinner, provided natural opportunities to do this. Through uncle George they caught up on recent events in Ireland, especially the movement for partial 'home rule' in which he was strongly involved, and the rise of Sinn Fein with its demand for an independent republic.

Just after Christmas newspapers reported on the successful overthrow of the Qing Government, and Dr Sun Yat-sen's election as President of the new Chinese Republic to begin on 1 January 1912.[29] The Stewarts knew that he had studied medicine and been baptized in Hong Kong, and believed that he was the right leader for such an historic change. Wondering how the change would impact missionary work in Szechwan, they looked forward to hearing from James and Mildred. Over the next few weeks, they heard that many working-class Chinese in Hong Kong had welcomed the

28. A. Stewart, After Seventy Years, 14–15.
29. *Irish News and Belfast Morning News*, 30 December 1911, 4.

revolution with a huge outburst of support, "feeling that since the Manchus had been driven out of China, the British should be next. Crowds looted shops, threw stones at the police, and tried to rescue prisoners in jail. Europeans rushed to purchase firearms after some were attacked on the streets."[30] Since wealthier Chinese in the Colony did not want to harm its economic and political stability, they preferred to maintain the status quo. The most tangible impact of the revolution was the large number of refugees coming across the border each day.

Towards the end of January, Philip, now a Captain, came home again on a two months leave from Malta.[31] Conversations ranged from Philip's latest travel to Italy, his lectures on hygiene to the troops, and medical breakthroughs for treating war wounds, to the pros and cons of life in the British colonies of Malta and Hong Kong. Evan showed real interest in Arthur and Kathleen's description of Chinese culture and work at St Paul's. After this visit, a letter came from James and Mildred saying that they had watched Sun Yat-sen's procession through Shanghai prior to his becoming President of the new Republic in Nanking. While waiting to hear about their return to Szechwan, James was asked to take part in a CMS National Conference to discuss the impact of the new political scene. He was also invited as a delegate to the International Missionary Council Conference with John Mott, which was seeking to form national associations of students for evangelism in China and India. Jim appreciated the opportunity to not only catch up again with his mentor but to get to know others involved in student work across Asia. While he was expecting to head back to Chengtu in April, as it was considered unsafe for women to resume their work for a time, Mildred arranged some temporary teaching at SSC in Hong Kong.

As part of his furlough, Arthur was often away on deputation. Along with talks on the continuing need for workers in China, he was also hoping to interest a few graduates in teaching at St Paul's to deal with its exploding enrolment. During the next eight months, he spoke at more than a hundred meetings. Kathleen sometimes accompanied him on these trips, joining him on the platform to talk about the importance of work among girls and women. In and around Dublin, she also spoke at a number of churches and ladies meetings.

On one occasion, when Arthur was lamenting the lack of response to the need for teachers at the College, Evan mentioned that for several years he had been thinking seriously about returning to China. He had planned

---

30. Carroll, *Concise History of Hong Kong*, 81–82.

31. Accounts of the first may be found in Killeen, *Short History of Ireland*, 78–94, and of the second in Lary, *China's Republic*, 14–44.

to go after graduating from TCD, but why couldn't he go back with them now and complete his degree later? Arthur was very open to the idea and saw how it would also provide Evan with a small income towards finishing his university studies.

Between engagements, Arthur was able to enjoy his favorite pastime, cycling, often covering large distances. This enabled him to see parts of Ireland within reach of Dublin, as well as improve his physical strength. When, at the end of his furlough, CMS's Medical Board asked if he was in shape to return to Hong Kong, he replied that he "had ridden 122 miles one day on a pushbike. They passed me as fit!"[32]

In late January 1913, the three Stewarts arrived in Hong Kong. When Evan stepped off the boat, the fifth Stewart had returned to China. Kathleen was no longer classified by CMS as a probationer but, as she was receiving a salary from the College, preferred the status of 'Local Missionary', giving her greater freedom to determine her field of work. Since they had been away, she and Arthur noticed several changes in the Colony. The large influx of refugees into overcrowded parts of the city; a consequent heightening of the annual risk of cholera during the summer months; an increasing number of vehicles on the roads; and the first buildings under construction in the new University precinct. At St Paul's, enrolments had continued to climb. Though this was good news, it meant that the Old Block had to be demolished and replaced with more modern premises to accommodate nearly 400 boys. As he began teaching, Evan had noticed the deteriorating condition of the old Diocesan premises used by the College: "Two enormous classrooms on the first floor and one on the ground floor—the rest of the space taken up with wide verandas and staircases, the whole constructed on ancient and somewhat worm-eaten wood, which must have caused a headache to the Insurance Company; the bad lighting and amazing discomforts which would not be tolerated by modern schoolboys."[33]

Since a small number of new students were coming from outside Hong Kong, a hostel to accommodate them was also rented near Government House. Its first housemaster, Wong Shiu Pun, whose English name was Preston, had become a Christian through Arthur and was now one of his closest friends. The increase in enrolments also meant the hiring of more teachers, several of whom were former students of SPC. On her return, Kathleen took on a full teaching load at St Paul's, including Matriculation English, being one of only two women on the staff. Along with a Vice-Principal, there were

32. A. Stewart, After Seventy Years, 15.
33. 'College History'. St Paul's College.

eight Masters, five of them Chinese. As well as teaching Maths and History, Evan was also a sports-master.

The curriculum contained a blend of academic and practical subjects, and its delivery was a mixture of formal and conversational learning. This approach was progressive for its day, especially in a Chinese context. In senior years students learned Modern World History; Geography; English Literature, Composition, and Letter-Writing; Mathematics including Arithmetic, Algebra, Stocks and Shares; Chinese Studies in History, Confucianism, Ethics, and Literature; Mandarin; Geometry as well as Scripture. [34]

By the close of the 1913 school year, the College's growing reputation for academic excellence was demonstrated by the fact that thirteen out of seventeen students passed the Oxford Local Examinations. At the same time, the College was also doing well in a variety of sports, such as Football and Volley Ball. In Athletics they secured prizes in the Hong Kong Schools Sports Carnival, partly due to Evan's coaching expertise. "The College soon earned a reputation for its remarkably proficient musicians and its Chinese plays", assisted by Kathleen's expertise in music and drama.[35] The Stewarts were encouraged that St Paul's was producing well-rounded students, some of whom were involved in the voluntary Scripture Union lunch-time group. Alongside weekly student-run bible talks, it also financially supported two Christian teachers in a country district.[36]

In his annual report for 1913, Arthur outlined three forward steps St Paul's was taking:

> In the first place we are seeking to make our education here as far as possible a commercial one. We try to do this by laying much stress on idiomatic English, especially spoken English, by object lessons and conversation lessons in the lower forms, and frequent debates in the upper forms: Book-keeping is taught in the higher forms and a shorthand class, formed two months ago, has been well attended. Now that we have laid in a supply of four typewriters, we hope for good results in this direction also.
>
> Another step we are taking is one which many of us have long felt to be of utmost importance, namely the opening of a boarding establishment in connection with this school. No one conversant with the condition of things prevailing in the student world of Hong Kong can but feel the importance of

34. This appeared in 'Prospectus St Paul's College, 1914', and was reported in *The Hong Kong Telegraph*, 15 December 1913, 4.

35. Fung, *From Devotion to Plurality*, 62.

36. For an account of Christian student groups in the College, see Fung, *From Devotion to Plurality*, 175–181.

opening places where they can be sheltered from the dangers that surround them, and receive that restraint and moral control so peculiarly necessary at their time of life. For the needs of the moment we are renting two houses in Caine Road capable of accommodating from twenty to twenty-five boarders. It is not an ideal arrangement, but we are hoping for something later on.

The third step is the opening of a Junior School in the middle of the town, with lower fees and a less advanced course of education. We are linking that school to this one by means of annual scholarships, so that promising scholars may be encouraged and helped to continue their studies. We are hoping to make it a training ground for some of our senior boys and at the same time, we hope to bring that moral and spiritual influence, which has meant so much to this school, to bear on a yet wider circle.[37]

Alongside his work at the College, Evan enlisted in the Hong Kong Artillery and Rifle Volunteer Corps. This home defence unit met British military standards, and took over the duties of regular army units when these had to be deployed elsewhere. Responsibilities included occasional guard duty, public parades, ongoing training, and occasional military exercises.

Kathleen enjoyed teaching the boys at the College but was aware that school-aged girls were missing out. She found that a number of families at St Paul's Church felt the same. Having had several years prior experience of girls education, she came to three main conclusions: there was a group of middle-class students not yet being reached by St Stephen's Girls College with its higher fees; instead of a number of one-teacher girls schools set up by missionaries who came and went, it would be better to have one ongoing centre; as well as evangelism taking place organically within the school, it should also be a base for reaching parents and others in the community. Kathleen's vision was to establish a low-fee paying, integrated curriculum, properly registered, College. St Paul's Church Vestry was willing to sponsor and support this proposal. With Arthur's assistance, she began to develop plans to open St Paul's Girls College [SPGC] the following year.

In the middle of 1914, when the Warden's position at St Stephen's College [SSC] fell vacant, Bishop Lander asked Arthur to become Principal of both institutions. His extraordinary success at St Paul's College was a major reason for this. Arthur was only able to do this because the schools were just a few miles apart. Since he was already holding down two positions—Principal of St Paul's College and Vicar of St Paul's Church—he handed over some of his responsibilities in the church to a Chinese assistant.

37. From the *Precis, South China Mission*, 1914, 3–4.

Children of the Massacre
大屠殺中倖存的孩子們

When James arrived back in Chengtu he oversaw the final stages of building the CMS hostel while waiting for the University to re-open. Although he had an English sub-Warden, Rev O. St M. Forester, James recruited a bright young student, Yen Chen Yee as his Chinese sub-Warden. The two of them soon formed a close personal and working partnership. Yen often translated for Jim, as he called him, who he introduced as Wen-Shuan Sze, which meant 'brilliant scholar.' James wrote:

> Among the objects we have in view [for the Hostel] are: (i) keeping in touch with the new education movement in Chengtu, (ii) working among the thousands of students in this great centre, who are at present utterly neglected, (iii) following up and shepherding young men from our own stations who go up to this provincial capital to complete their studies or for other purposes.[38]

James at the Student Hostel, Chengtu

38. *Bulletin of the Diocese*, November 1913, 6–7.

In the second half of 1912, Mildred, having done "valuable work in the CMS School in Hong Kong", returned to Szechwan.[39] Instead of going back to Chung-pa, she was appointed to teach at the CMS Girls Boarding School in Mienchuh. This focussed on educating primary aged girls from the surrounding district but also taught day students from within the city. Increasingly fluent in Mandarin, she was also able to build good relationships with parents through home visits.

Being in Mienchuh also gave her opportunity to see more of Reg Taylor. In the summer, at the annual conference in the mountains, the two of them decided they were open to more than friendship. This commitment was important since Mil, as he called her, had been appointed to work in Chongkiang, which was south-east from Mienchuh and a day's journey from Chengtu.

At the university hostel in Chengtu, Y. C. Yen was proving so helpful that "such promise should not be contained in a landlocked city in Szechwan . . . [James] felt strongly that Yen should be given opportunity for higher education even though it meant a real loss to himself."[40] He believed that Yen had an indispensable part to play in the leadership and mission of the whole church in Szechwan. James recommended that Yen undertake University overseas study, and that the best place to prepare for this would be in Hong Kong. In the summer, Jim traveled the long distance there with him. Arthur suggested that St Stephen's was most academically geared for this. Although matriculation usually took up to three year's study, Yen managed to complete the work in just six months. His "remarkable scholastic progress was due in large part to the happy hours he spent with the Stewarts, and especially to the stimulating and inspiring friendship he had with James."[41]

Shortly after James returned to Chengtu, he reported:

> We are getting a nice number of students coming this term, as we have nearly fifty in our Evening Classes. They arrive about 4pm and go on to 7pm . . . I am getting great pleasure out of my classes in the Government Schools. I have four in all, with about a hundred and fifty students. They are most delightful to teach, especially in the English Conversation classes, when I am free to choose my own subject . . . Next Friday at the hostel I am having an Evening for students . . . We have changed our Sunday night preaching into a more Evangelistic Service . . . Last Sunday we were crowded out.[42]

39. *Bulletin of the Diocese*, October 1912, 18.
40. Brochure of Rev James Stewart Memorial Fellowship, column 2.
41. Brochure of Rev James Stewart Memorial Fellowship, column 3.
42. *Bulletin of the Diocese*, 8 March, 22–23.

According to the Anglican Bishop, William Cassels: "His lectures at the YMCA. on 'Christianity and Evolution' were attended by 300 or 400 students, and on one occasion he was invited to give a lecture to an association of teachers and students, at which the attendance was fully 500. He much enjoyed speaking to them on 'The Truth shall make you free.'"[43]

At the beginning of 1914, James reported further growth in the student work at the hostel. Previously it had only been able to accommodate up to ten students, but now there was space for nearly forty. Concerned to maintain the quality of relationships, he only wanted to add students slowly. The strategy was to encourage the Christians to invite their friends to 'open houses'. The English Bible Class had grown to twelve. There were now Sunday afternoon talks on topical issues, a small library containing Bibles and books from a Christian perspective, and a reading room with free Christian literature.

Reg going to propose to Mildred

43. Cassels was one of the famous 'Cambridge Seven', and the first bishop in West China. His story is contained in Pollack, *Cambridge Seven* and the quote comes from *Bulletin of the Diocese*, April 1916, 3.

In March, James received news from Mildred that she and Reg had just become engaged. Reg had ridden a day and a night, dressed in his best outfit, on a mountain pony adorned with a garland of bells, "to take the engagement ring to my Love in her station at Chongkiang."[44] By mid-year, James reported to Bishop Cassels that there were now twenty hostellers in residence, and about eighty young men attending the Bible Classes. "If we had a stronger staff we could develop considerably. I have refused applications both for residence and for entrance to our classes, as I feel that with our present staff we cannot manage anymore."[45]

James was honored by being asked to give the final thanksgiving address at the upcoming Diocesan Council Conference. "It was", as Cassels remarked, "always a great pleasure to see him, because he had won our hearts in a peculiar way, and was always a strength to our gathering."

In early August, James organized a fortnight's holiday for himself, Milly, her fiancée Reg, Dr and Mrs Lechler, at their summer house in the mountains. "The temperature was very cool, and sometimes magnificent views could be obtained. Unfortunately, however, brigands were reported to be in the mountains, and the officials became anxious, so it seemed well to return to the station."[46]

A few weeks later, an Irish newspaper reported that:

> On 2 September 1914, at Mienchuh in the province of Szechwan, the Rev Reginald Charles Taylor and Miss Mildred Eleanor Stewart were united in the bonds of Holy Matrimony. The Rev H. H. Taylor performed the ceremony . . . and gave a short and practical address based on the words 'Heirs together of the Grace of God'. The service took place in the church which was especially decorated by the Chinese for the occasion. . . . Among the crowded congregation the most important visitors were the Chi Si with members of his staff and the ladies from the Yamen.
>
> The Bridegroom was supported by Dr Lechler and the Rev J. R. Stewart gave away the blushing bride whose [Irish] wedding gown had a foundation of white silk, with an overdress of chiffon edged with Carricknacross lace. [The organist] played the Wedding March, and a Chinese Band discoursed sweet music at intervals. Owing to the present political situation many friends were prevented from being present at the happy event . . . After the ceremony Dr and Mrs Lechler held an elegant reception in their home, and disbursed liberal hospitality to all the

---

44. From the family album of their grandson, David Taylor
45. For this and the following quote see again *Bulletin of the Diocese*, April 1916, 3.
46. *Bulletin of the Diocese*, September 1914, 19.

assembled guests ... after which Mr and Mrs Taylor left amid a shower of good wishes, for Teh-yang and Chengtu ... [47]

This event was partly overshadowed by the news that war had broken out in Europe. The ensuing four-year conflict was to have a decisive impact on all the Stewarts.

---

47. *Daily Mail*, 3 September 1914, no page.

4

Experiences of Loss and Love (1914–1925)

AT THE OUTBREAK OF the Great War, Philip was stationed at Tidworth Military Base Hospital in England. Located on the sprawling Salisbury Plain in south-east Wiltshire, this was a major center for the Royal Army's Southern Command. This now became a major training ground for newly recruited troops from all over the British Empire heading to Europe. The British Expeditionary Force [BEF], as it was called, included contingents from Canada, Australia, New Zealand and other Dominions.

On 13 August, Philip's regiment boarded ship in Southampton for France. In his 3rd Worcestershire 2nd Battalion, there were twenty-six officers, nearly a thousand other ranks, and sixty horses. After an overnight stay in the port of Le Havre, they steamed:

> ... up the Seine, with its vistas of rolling forests and picturesque Norman villages. The inhabitants on the banks cheered the troops, and excitement on board ran high. At 9 p.m. the Battalion disembarked on the broad quays of Rouen, where they passed the night ... Early next morning [it] marched through the streets to the station and entrained for the Front. The five days which followed were very trying. The weather was hot. Officers and men became accustomed to long periods of travelling in sluggish jolting troop trains, to sleeping anywhere they could lay their heads, and to apparently needless marching and counter-marching ... [1]

1. From the 3rd Battalion Worcestershire Regiment website. At https://www.

Philip in full military dress

The battalion alighted from the trains on 16 August. Over the next week, it marched forty- two miles towards Mons, where the first shell of Philip's war shrieked overhead and burst behind him. On arrival, the troops were billeted for several days in nearby villages while they undertook final training, inspections, and practice marches. Shortly after reaching the Front, the battalion was engaged in the Battle of Mons, the first major action of the British Army on European soil since the Battle of Waterloo against Napoleon. Four divisions of the BEF attempted to hold the line against the advancing German 1st Army across the twenty-yard wide Mons Canal. Although the British fought well, and inflicted disproportionate casualties on the numerically superior enemy, the sudden retreat of the French 5th Army on 24 August forced them to withdraw. This action lasted two weeks and

worcestershireregiment.com.

took them to the outskirts of Paris, before the Allied forces counter-attacked near the river Marne and, by 12 September, temporarily ended the German advance.

During this action, Philip's work as Regimental Medical Officer

> ... began at a rudimentary care point within two to three hundred yards of the front line. Regimental Aid Posts [RAP] were set up in small spaces such as communication trenches, ruined buildings, dug outs, or a deep shell hole. The walking wounded struggled to make their way to these, whilst more serious cases were carried by comrades or sometimes stretcher bearers. The RAP had no holding capacity and here, often in appalling conditions, wounds would be cleaned and dressed, pain relief administered and basic first aid given. The Regimental Medical Officer in charge was supplied equipment such as anti-tetanus serum, bandages, field dressings, cotton wool, ointments and blankets ... as well as comforts such as brandy, cocoa and biscuits. If possible, men were returned to their duties but the more seriously wounded were carried by ... stretcher bearers, often over muddy and shell-pocked ground, and under shell fire, to the Advanced Dressing Station.[2]

The next phase of this conflict, described as 'The Race to the Sea', took place from 17 September to 19 October. During this struggle, the German and Allied armies tried to outflank and attack each other from the rear. At stake was the fate of the Channel Ports and their vital communications with Great Britain. This 'cat-and-mouse' contest took them both north towards the Belgian frontier, and towards the shores of the North Sea. It was the Allied forces who finally managed to hold the ground near Arras and Bapaume in northern France.

On 19 October, a new German offensive began just over the border in the Belgian town of Langemark. The lengthy 'First Battle of Ypres', as this was called, proved to be the last major battle of 1914. Unfortunately, on the third day of action, Philip was wounded, suffering "a rifle bullet to his chest, sustaining a severe, but non-permanent injury."[3] His family in Ireland heard this news the next day when the War Office's casualty list was published in the press. It seems most likely that Philip was evacuated to the Base Hospital in Boulogne for surgery and rehabilitation.

From the outbreak of War, James had thought about using his upcoming furlough to serve as a temporary chaplain in the army. Though, for the

---

2. 'Evacuation of the Wounded'. History Press.
3. RAMC Officers, 2.

time being, China itself remained neutral and, as a clergyman, he was exempt from military service, hearing about Philip's injury only strengthened his resolve. As his friend C. Y. Yen remarked: "He could not remain idle while his Motherland was engaged in War, losing thousands of men every day."[4] Leaving Chengtu in February 1915, he headed to the coast, catching a ship to Singapore en route to the UK. Having made up his mind to enlist, he decided to fast-track this by activating the Officer Training he had undertaken several years before at Sydney University. As Singapore was a British colony, he was able there to join the Australian Army Chaplains' Department, attached to Philip's battalion in the Worcestershire Regiment. Back onboard ship, he learned the devastating news about the slaughter of both Australasian and British troops on the Gallipoli peninsula in Turkey.

Arriving in England on Monday 24 May, he was only there for five days before leaving for France.[5] On disembarking in Boulogne, James found himself Chaplain to two thousand wounded men being cared for in Base Hospitals and nearby Convalescent Camps.[6] Though having seen much hardship in China, especially during natural disasters and regular epidemics, he was not prepared for the sight of so many wounded and dying young men. As Chaplain, James took seriously the charge he had been given.

> "Helping the sick . . . is an art which needs careful judgment in each individual case. Many of these men, especially those recently wounded, are suffering from shock, and require quietening and reassurance. Many of them are anxious to send messages to relatives and those dear to them . . . if you are attached to a military hospital visit the patients regularly and constantly, . . . your work . . . should be a help and not a hindrance to that of the medical officers, and it is your task to give calmness, cheerfulness, and courage as much as you can. But sometimes, in cases that are hopeless, you may be able to break the gravest tidings. That will require all your wisdom, tenderness and fortitude."[7]

In mid-summer, James was posted to the regiment's headquarters in Flanders. Here, as 'padre', he worked mainly among able-bodied officers and supporting ranks. One of his main responsibilities was organizing regular services and participating in occasional parades. On these occasions, he

---

4. *Bulletin of the Diocese*, April 1916, 8.
5. *West Australian*, 4 May 1917, 8.
6. 'Beyond 1914', University of Sydney.
7. Though this comes from a later document, it reflects the advice of an early Anglican chaplain of the AIF, and may be found in Tippett, 'Australian Army Chaplains', 329.

sought to speak about Christianity in ways that were relevant to everyday life in the army with its concerns, fears, hopes, and longings. He made sure that prayers were informal and down-to-earth, and that hymns were connected to issues that were real for the men.

In early autumn, James wrote to Yen, that:

> "He was at first about thirty miles from the firing-line, but . . . that there he could scarcely get in touch with the soldiers, for whom especially he went. So finally, in some mysterious way, he succeeded in obtaining special permission to go right to the front, into the trenches . . . [There] he was Chaplain of a Brigade consisting of 6,000 soldiers, and 'I spend my time going around the trenches and billets, and holding services, talking with men, or else visiting the ambulances, when the wounded and dying are being attended to. It is often very sad work, but it gives me many opportunities of speaking about Christ's love, and I am glad I came'."[8]

大屠殺中倖存的孩子們

Evan returned to Ireland in the middle of 1915. Initially, he planned to resume his studies at TCD after the summer. But, as allied fatalities mounted into the tens of thousands, he increasingly felt compelled to volunteer. Though as an undergraduate he was exempt from military service, the number of his Wellington College friends in the forces demonstrated that "everyone who was anything 'went to the war.'"[9] As soon as Evan reached the UK he enlisted. Having already completed Officer Training at Wellington, and served with the HKVDC, he was immediately commissioned as 2nd Lieutenant. Evan offered to train for the relatively new and dangerous work of being a machine gunner and was seconded to the Middlesex Regiment which specialized in this kind of warfare.[10] Since there was a close link between the regiment and Wellington College, this arrangement suited him perfectly.

Evan was sent to the regiment's base in Aldershot, south-east from London, for his training. This involved long hours of learning the mechanics

---

8. *Bulletin of the Diocese*, April 1916, 8.

9. Recalled by Dr Peter Ride, in Stewart, *Hong Kong Volunteer Corps*, Appendix VIII. The writer is the grandchild of Arthur and Margaret Stewart. The proportion of space accorded to the Roll of Honour in the Wellington College Year Book for 1914 revealed this dramatically.

10. Based on personal correspondence with Evan's son, Colonel Michael Stewart.

of how to assemble, operate, position, maintain, and transport this complex, at times unreliable, weapon over different types of terrain. Since it required four to six men to operate—one to fire, one to feed the ammunition, and the rest to carry the cumbersome weapon, belts of cartridges, and spare parts—this also involved leading and inspiring a team. From accounts of early battles in the war, he learned about the "deadly results" that came from both concentrated bursts, or continuous rounds, of machine gun fire on the advancing enemy.[11]

After his training finished, Evan left Southampton to join the battalion in northern France where they had already fought in two significant battles. In March, at Neuve Chapelle, British and Indian soldiers, with the aid of its machine guns, managed to hold their ground in the face of a German counter-attack and take around seventeen hundred prisoners. In May, with French support, the regiment tried to take Aubers Ridge, but this proved to be a disaster, with the British Army suffering over ten thousand casualties on the first day.

It was during a periodic lull in the fighting that Evan arrived. These were the early days of trench warfare—before steel helmets, pill-boxes, tanks, and when bombs were made out of jam-tins, and mortars from gas-pipes. Trenches themselves were only temporary positions, not places to live, 'manned' by regiments rostered for limited periods. Most of the time troops were billeted in houses, schools, farms, and barns in nearby towns and villages. Behind the front line there were rifle inspections, arms drills, field exercises—at times also cricket and rugby matches between regiments, and polo games between officers! Sometimes soldiers walked a few kilometers into Bethune to the public baths for a wash, cafés for a snack, hotels for a drink, or to one of the many French brothels.

On 25 September, as part of the largest British attack of the war that year, Evan's regiment was to lead the advance in its section of the battle of Loos. This began with a forty-minute gas-attack on the Germans, which went ahead despite advice that wind shifts could blow it back on British lines. A soldier in a nearby regiment described what happened that first day:

> We heard ... a distant cheer, the confused crackle of rifle fire, yells, heavy shelling on our front line ... and a continuous rattle of machine guns. After a few minutes, lightly wounded men of the Middlesex came stumbling down ... to the dressing-station ... 'What's happened? I asked. 'Bloody balls-up' was the most detailed answer I could get. Among the wounded were a number

---

11. Cornish, 'Machine Gun'. See further this author's full-length account of 'the machine gun and the Great War' in his book with this title.

of men yellow-faced and choking, with their buttons tarnished green; these were gas cases. Then came the stretcher cases. [After this] two companies of the Middlesex . . . instead of waiting for the intense bombardment which was to follow . . . charged . . . and got as far as the German wire—which our artillery had not attempted to cut. The Germans shot them down . . . Two other companies . . . soon followed in support. Machine-gun fire stopped them half-way.[12]

For this attack, Evan's unit consisted of four machine guns co-ordinated to create a denser field of fire during attack or retreat. In the chaos of battle, he came to realize the importance of leading by example—remaining calm under attack, showing confidence in his men, and developing esprit de corps. Since machine gun batteries operated from exposed positions unsupported by other troops, they were especially vulnerable to concentrated fire from the enemy. This is why such units were described with the macabre label 'suicide clubs.'

That day, the Middlesex suffered over five hundred casualties, including eleven officers, but that night held the line. Along the whole front, British casualties were eight thousand strong, and, by the end of the main attack, growing to fifty thousand, with a further ten thousand in subsidiary attacks over the next two weeks. The battle of Loos was a disaster for the Allied Forces and ended military operations for 1915 while the generals worked out their next strategy. During this time, life returned to the pattern of short spells 'on watch' in the trenches, with the 'new normal' behind the lines only occasionally interrupted by shelling. "It was as though there had been no battle except that the Senior Officers were fewer and the Special Reserve larger."[13]

James' battalion was a little further down the line from the Middlesex. During this conflict he showed conspicuous bravery, not just through his care for the men but through going beyond his Chaplain's duties to serve as a stretcher-bearer under fire.[14] After the battle, the two brothers were able to meet up in the nearby village of Bois Grenier.[15] This 'chance' meeting probably took place in the village which, though largely abandoned, still had a bakery as well as a hotel that served meals. Having not seen each other for seven years, both felt this meeting was providential. It took James a while to

12. The writer was the renowned author Robert Graves, in his *Goodbye To All That*, 196–7, 199–200, 207, a renowned memoir of the First World War.

13. Graves, *Goodbye to All That*, 209.

14. *Bulletin of the Diocese*, April 1916, 3–4.

15. From a family document provided by Michael Stewart.

get used to seeing Evan as an adult in military uniform. Time seemed to pass too quickly as they talked about the battle and caught up with recent family news. As they said goodbye, James prayed for them both.

Evan in early years of the war

The remainder of 1915 was largely a period of stalemate in which both sides 'dug in' and lived in trenches. For James and other Chaplains, this involved "burying scores, sometimes hundreds of men a day. Theirs was the sad task of bundling up the few pathetic treasures of the dead, the writing of letters to the next of kin, and trying to put into those letters some humanity to soften the starkness of official telegrams nobody wanted to deliver."[16] Just after Christmas, under constant shellfire on the Front, James showed his

---

16. Tippett, 'Army Chaplains', 326.

Experiences of Loss and Love (1914–1925)

continuing concern and prayer for his students in Chengtu. As he wrote to one young man:

> I was grieved to hear that your mother was still so opposed to Christianity, and so anxious for you to give it up. No one can understand what the presence of Christ means until they have felt the joy of speaking with Him, and of knowing that His message is true, that God is indeed our Father, watching over us and caring for us, grieving when we go astray and seeking to guide us . . .I feel sure that as you persevere your mother will come to see that your faith in Christ has helped you to lead a better and more unselfish life. I pray often that God will use you to help her to see the Truth.[17]

On Sunday evening, 2 January, the Senior Chaplain of the BEF was due to officiate at a burial but unexpectedly invited by his superior to address a service for soldiers in Bethune four miles away. James felt this was too good an opportunity to miss, and offered to take the burial for him. As he was conducting the funeral at Cambrin, close to the line, shells started to come over from enemy lines, wounding an officer and several men, but striking James in the head and killing him instantly.

The following day, the Worcestershire Regiment recorded the death of their Chaplain who was: "beloved by all, nothing was too much trouble, and no risk daunted him. He is remembered for his bravery at Loos."[18] At his funeral, on 4 January, the Senior Chaplain of the BEF, stated:

> It was an unselfish death. He undertook this funeral to save me . . . Mr Stewart was universally respected and loved by officers and men, especially by those with whom he lived and knew him best . . . [His] friends at home and abroad can rest assured that he had finished the work God had given him to do . . . and perhaps some will be moved to offer themselves for the vacant place in the Mission Field.[19]

James was laid to rest in Bethune Town Cemetery alongside others from his regiment. On 18 January, CMS in the UK recorded that James: " . . . had already won his way into many hearts by his loving personality, and also had won the great respect of all who knew him as an able and valued

---

17. *Bulletin of the Diocese*, April 1916, 2.
18. Worcestershire WW1 Centenary.
19. *Bulletin of the Diocese*, April 1916, 5.

missionary, his fellow missionaries (and especially his Bishop) having come to look upon him as full of promise as a leader for the future."²⁰

Soldiers' graves in Bethune Town Cemetery

大屠殺中倖存的孩子們

For Kathleen, the beginning of 1915 brought the long-awaited opening of the Girls College, with fifty students.²¹ Premises were found in a spacious rented building at 2 Caine Road, further uphill from St Paul's Church. In contrast to St Stephen's Girls School, the College was set up to provide a Christian-based education for Chinese girls from poor families. It offered curricula from Kindergarten to Junior Secondary School. Boys were also enrolled until Year 4 when they transferred to SPC. A unique feature was the use of Cantonese as the medium for all instruction. The College's motto, 'Faith, Hope, and Love', from 1 Corinthians 13:13, summed up both its ethos and intention.

Even before SPGC opened, Kathleen was experiencing muscle pains, night sweats, tiredness, and weight loss, but put it down to the pressure of overwork. Consultations with the doctor were at first inconclusive, but later she was diagnosed with tuberculosis, then mostly a life-threatening disease. Frustratingly for Kathleen, a return to Ireland for specialized treatment

---

20. Minute from the Parent Committee, 18 January 1916.
21. See further Barker, *Change and Continuity*, 34–35.

and complete rest was strongly recommended. Her unexpected departure meant that over the summer a replacement had to be found. Providentially, Dr Catherine Woo had just returned from studies at Oxford University to Hong Kong. Coming from a strong Christian and medical family and being deeply committed to the importance of women's education, CMS recommended her for the position. This made her the first Chinese female school principal in Hong Kong.[22]

Kathleen arrived in Dublin only a couple of months after the so-called Easter Rebellion had traumatized the city. Over six days, one and a half thousand armed Nationalists seized several important buildings, shot local police and soldiers without warning, and proclaimed an Irish republic. British reinforcements and artillery were brought in to attack the rebels, and vicious fighting took place. The shelling and resulting fires caused carnage on the streets of Dublin and left parts of the city in ruins. Nearly five hundred people, many of them civilians, were killed and several times that number wounded. In May, sixteen of the rebel leaders were executed. Though some members of Kathleen's wider family lived close to much of the fighting, fortunately they were unharmed. Being a distance away in Monkstown, aunt Tem was largely protected from the conflict. However, the insurrection "transformed many Irish people's attitudes to independence and set in train a series of events that would lead to the partition of Ireland" in 1922.[23]

After tests, it was found that Kathleen was not suffering from tuberculosis but a case of untreated malaria. However, she was also discovered to have an 'internal tumor' requiring an immediate operation. This surgery was successful, but her recovery took some time.

When James left for the front, CMS asked the Taylors to temporarily take charge of the Student Hostel in the University in Chengtu. Over the following months, they had received correspondence from James about his ministry on the Front. When news of his death reached them, Mildred was heartbroken at having lost her closest brother. She recalled how thoughtful and protective Jim had been towards her in the last few years, and sad that she would never be able to introduce him to their son, Lionel, who was born two months before he died. When Reg told the students at the Hostel, they were shaken and visibly distressed. At a Memorial Service attended by fellow missionaries, university staff, and students, Bishop Cassels summed up the reaction of everyone who knew him: "He literally and actually died as he

---

22. Heritage Impact Assessment Report, February 2011.

23. 'Easter Rising', History Extra. The Rebellion was commemorated in W. B. Yeats's moving poem, 'Easter 1916', *Collected Poems of W. B. Yeats,* three of whose four stanzas close with the haunting line "a terrible beauty is born". On the whole incident and its repercussions, see Bunbury, *Easter Dawn.*

had lived, in service—in the service of God and man—and to us it seemed that his service had only just begun when he was called away."[24]

At the hostel, Reg was pleased to be back in a university environment. Students appreciated the family-like atmosphere to which Milly and baby Lionel contributed, especially when they were feeling homesick. Unfortunately, not long into their work, Reg had an acute attack of appendicitis requiring an urgent operation and was only able to fully resume his duties after several months convalescing. One of the outstanding graduates of West China Christian Union University that Reg nurtured during his time at the hostel was Song Cheng-Tsi. Though, as a university student, he was mentored by James, militant family opposition had prevented him from being publicly baptised. By the time the Taylors got to know him, he was married and had a child. Mildred befriended his wife, encouraged her developing faith, and helped guide her as a young mother. As Reg wrote: "I baptized him in 1916. He came to Christ through Jim Stewart, read the Bible through and through, and endured much persecution from his mother to whom he was devoted."[25] Milly and Reg then went on to spend three more years working at the CMS Hostel in Chengtu.

As Arthur—'A.D.' to his colleagues and friends—prepared for the 1915 academic year, to his great delight an increase in applications led to three hundred and fifty enrolments at the College. He was grateful that staff morale remained high, and for the way teachers gave of themselves to help the boys in their spare time, and took on extra work when asked. This year, instead of teachers running a weekly after-school Scripture Union group, Arthur said that the boys now organized meetings. Another highlight was three Old Boys of the College seeking his advice about where they should train for the ministry.

Aware that his health was suffering due to the pressure of work, and concerned about Kathleen, Arthur decided to apply for an early, shorter, furlough. This was agreed to, and he arrived back in Ireland in February 1917. Though it was a relief to see Kathleen up and about, she was still a long way from her usual energetic self. The prognosis was that full recovery would take at least another year. Catching up with uncle George, who had recently become Governor of the Bank of Ireland, gave Arthur opportunity to discuss the financial aspects of a future building program for the College. Staying at aunt Tem's also gave him time to broach with Kathleen his desire to court the bishop's elder daughter, Kitty Lander. As he was almost forty,

---

24. *Bulletin of the Diocese*, 15 April 1916, 1–2.
25. From family material provided by Reg and Mildred's grandson, David Taylor.

Experiences of Loss and Love (1914–1925) 83

and she only in her early twenties, he wondered whether the age-gap was too large. Having got to know Kitty, Kathleen thought it was a great idea!

Mildred and Lionel with Mrs Song (on right)

By the end of July 1917, he was on his way back to Hong Kong, via Canada. In early December, the Taylors stayed for a time at the beginning of their furlough. Since Mildred was heavily pregnant with their second child, they were planning to be in Hong Kong for the birth. During this visit, they talked a lot about James, whose estate was bequeathed to CMS for additional staff residences at the Hostel in Chengtu. Mildred also caught up with friends and ex-students from her time at St Stephen's Girl School six years earlier. Just after Chinese New Year, Kathleen, named after her aunt, was born. In April 1918, the Taylors set off on the next leg of their furlough to Canada where, like Robert and Louisa twenty-five years earlier, they spent several months doing deputation work for CMS. The final stage of their furlough would be occupied with further deputation in the UK, seeking support for outreach to remote tribespeople, including Tibetans, in the north-west of Szechwan. This time would give them a chance to meet each other's families for the first time, as well as visit Kathleen in Ireland.

Not very much is known in detail about Philip and Evan's military service during the remaining years of the war, except that their battalions were involved in most of the major battles on the Western Front. In 1917, Philip, now a Temporary Major, was in charge of a Field Ambulance Unit, a mobile hospital acting as a midway point between regimental aid posts on the front line, and casualty clearing stations on the coast. Somewhere around this time he and Evan managed to meet up, but it is unclear exactly where this took place. Then:

> In April 1917 the first batch of over 1,000 Chinese volunteers arrived in France as the first recruits to the new Chinese Labour Corps (CLC). Although native Chinese English language students accompanied the CLC, the British Army was still scoured for Chinese language speakers. As Evan's home address was given as Hong Kong, they incorrectly assumed that he spoke Chinese. He was commissioned into the CLC as a Temporary 2nd Lieutenant on 24 July 1917, but as soon as practicable he arranged a transfer back to the Middlesex Regiment where he served the rest of the war.[26]

Evan was wounded twice by shrapnel, once in the left shoulder, and once requiring him to convalesce in Dublin before returning to the Front. A few fragments of shrapnel remained in his body for the rest of his life. In the final year of the war, the Middlesex was involved in the battles of Messines, Hazebrouck, St Quentin, Cambrai, and the Selle. After the Armistice, he was again seconded to the CLC, assisting a battalion to eventually travel back to China, and then demobilisze in Shanghai. He was awarded the British War and Victory Medals and, towards the end of his time with the Army, had become acting Major.[27]

For Kathleen, visiting Evan during his recovery in hospital encouraged her to undertake some basic nursing training which would also be useful on her return to St Paul's College.[28] She had delayed this because of the flu

26. From text accompanying Evan's medals, provided by Michael Stewart.

27. See further Record Details for Evan George Stewart, Forces War Records.

28. Kathleen describes her occupation as a 'nurse' when she was eventually able to set out for Hong Kong. See 'Atsuta Manu', Outward Bound Passenger Lists 1890–1960,

pandemic that had begun to sweep Ireland. The so-called 'Spanish Flu' first appeared there in June 1918. Three months later a second wave hit, closing schools, suburbs, and businesses in Dublin. The deadliest wave struck in February 1919 with the return of troops from France. As there was no medical consensus about the most effective treatment, victims tried a range of remedies including beef teas, tonics, and non-prescription medicines. Ultimately rest and good nursing brought about the best results. With many experienced nurses succumbing to the flu, however, women enrolled in training courses or stepped in as untrained volunteers. When, a few months later, the pandemic had finally run its course, a fifth of the population had caught it, and more than twenty thousand had died, mainly young adults.[29]

大屠殺中倖存的孩子們

Original site of St Paul's College

---

13 December 1919.

29. A well-researched recent novel, featuring a volunteer nurse, that depicts the pandemic in Ireland is Donaghue, *Pull of The Stars*.

During the previous year in Hong Kong, Arthur "saw a good deal of Kitty Lander . . . and we became engaged in April 1918."[30] Since Kitty would soon be traveling with her parents for their furlough in Canada, for a time the pair would have to be separated. During these lonely months, Arthur threw himself into the work of the College. With enrolments increasing every year, Lander had tacitly agreed to Arthur's proposal that the spacious Bishop's House and grounds be redeveloped into a larger hostel for boarders, and extra buildings for day students, in all catering for up to 500 students. All the Bishop asked was that his new residence be located on Victoria Peak. As CMS was unwilling to provide funding for this, Arthur's pursued a two-fold strategy. First, he asked the Chinese community if they would be willing to cover the cost of building a new hostel for 80 students, himself and wife, and three teachers on the site of the old College gardens. Second, with uncle George's help, he approached his wealthy relations in Ireland to raise the additional money needed to complete the project. Arthur took the risk of signing the contract to begin before all the funds were secured and the Bishop had returned from Canada. He did this, as he said, believing "I have the best of security; faith in my fellow-man, and faith in God." On arriving back in Hong Kong, Lander remarked jokingly that "he felt somewhat like a dog running after a motor car," and that, as the Bishop's House would soon be occupied by the school, "the Bishop will have nowhere to stay!" Throughout the consequent, sometimes complex, discussions with both CMS and the Diocese, it was recorded how much Arthur "stands by the school. It is his very life." [31]

On 11 November 1918 Germany signed the Armistice and hostilities ceased in all theatres of the War. Although the conflict had not greatly affected Hong Kong, it showed the Chinese how barbaric the 'civilized' West could be, and raised questions about the ultimate legitimacy of colonialism. Among the Stewarts, Philip stayed on as a doctor in the Regular Army and after a brief time in Malta was posted to Iraq.

After completing his time with the CLS in Shanghai, Evan decided to postpone completing his degree in Dublin and instead return to St Paul's in Hong Kong. Arthur was delighted when CMS approved this, commending him as a "missionary of the Society in Local Connection without financial responsibility. He has wonderful influence among Chinese students and is

---

30. A. Stewart, After Seventy Years, 15.

31. These quotes come from the South China Mission Original Papers, 1918–19, 2 January 1919 and from Yueng, Streams of Life, 20. On the development of the College at this time, see also the report in the South China Morning Post, 20 January 1919, 8, 12.

Experiences of Loss and Love (1914–1925) 87

whole-hearted in his devotion to the work. He might well be left in charge at St Paul's when his brother goes on furlough."³².

On January 25 1919, Arthur and Kitty were married by her father at St John's Cathedral. Among the wider family, Kathleen was disappointed that her passage to Hong Kong could not be arranged in time for the wedding. It wasn't until later in 1919 that she finally arrived, returning with the Taylors who, after a short stay, continued on to Shanghai and then Szechwan. It was a sad trip for all of them as, shortly before they left London, they heard the heart-breaking news that on 22 October Arthur and Kitty's first-born son had died.

Out of courtesy to her successor, Dr Woo, at the Girls College, after several years away Kathleen felt it best not to resume teaching there but join her brothers at SPC. She was keen, however, to see first-hand how the new school was faring. By 1920, its growth had required moving several times, most recently into premises at 47 Caine Road. A new curriculum had been introduced, including Physical Education and Home Economics. To minimize class distinctions, the Girls College became the first educational institution in Hong Kong to mandate wearing a school uniform. Another development was the adoption of such extra-curricular activities as dancing, drama, and singing.

Not long after her return, Kathleen met up again with Rev Ernest Martin, a fellow CMS missionary. Their paths had crossed briefly before she had to leave the Colony. A clergyman's son from County Durham, and a graduate of Clare College, Cambridge, at the time he was Chaplain at St Stephen's College. In 1917 he enlisted as a regular soldier in the CLC, and was given command of its 111th Company. Ernest took on the added responsibilities of teaching his mostly illiterate men to read, and of caring for the spiritual needs of Christians in his charge. After helping the CLC repatriate back to Shandong in 1919, Ernest, by then a Captain, returned to Hong Kong, and took up his chaplaincy at St Stephen's. Evan, having been awarded the British and Victory Medals for his service, completed his assignment with the CLC and returned to Hong Kong. After a short break from his service in the Regular Army, he re-joined the HKVDC. In Hong Kong, Ernest and Evan were drawn together through their common experience with the CLC and on the Western Front. This gave Kathleen opportunity to see more of Ernest and, as the year progressed, they developed a good friendship. In early March, "amid general rejoicing", their engagement was announced.³³

---

32. South China Mission Precis Book, 1918–1919, 2.
33. South China Mission Original Paper 1920–22, 7 March 1921.

Three Stewarts (1st row, center) with staff in 1920

At St Paul's, staff and students greatly appreciated having Evan, Arthur, and Kathleen together again in the College. Around this time, they heard from Y. C. Yen who, since graduating from Yale and Princeton, had also worked after the war among the Chinese Labour Corps in France with the International YMCA. While there, he was determined to search for James' grave in Bethune.

> "I had great difficulty in locating it, because there was no record kept anywhere in the vicinity. A friend and I went to see the mayor, who said he did not know anything about it, but there were some forty cemeteries around Bethune. I was in despair. Finally, we had to resort to the process of looking for the grave from cemetery to cemetery till we could locate it. So we agreed to start with the one right in the city. We were still worrying about the matter when the car stopped at the military section of the cemetery. The wonderful thing was that no sooner had the car stopped than my friend's chauffer called out at the top of his voice: 'What is that cross?' It was no other than the cross on Rev J. R. Stewart's grave. I almost broke down with the sudden joy and relief at finding it. It would have been my life's regret if I

had been to France and failed to see the grave of my heroic and Christlike friend."³⁴

In the spring of 1920, when Bishop Lander retired to England, a search was conducted for his successor. Arthur's was one of three names put forward but the position ultimately went to Charles Ridley Duppuy who had been a Chaplain on the Western Front. When he arrived in Hong Kong, the Stewart brothers were part of a small, select welcome party that greeted him on the ship and accompanied him by military launch and then sedan chairs³⁵ to the Bishop's House. A few weeks later, on 17 October, Kitty gave birth to twin sons, who were baptized Gerald Lander and Robert James. This wonderful news seemed to make up for the tragic loss of the year before. However, on 3 December a circular was sent to all the missionaries in Hong Kong: "You will be very grieved to hear that the twin sons of the Rev and Mrs A. D. Stewart both died on the 1st . . . We fear for the effect on Mrs Stewart after losing the elder son last year . . . up to the last we heard, they seemed to be doing well."³⁶ Insisting, for the sake of their health, that they needed to go away for a prolonged rest, CMS suggested the two take an early furlough. In spring 1921, with Evan placed in charge of the College, they left for the UK via Australia. Arriving in Sydney, they visited some of the places connected with James, such as Sydney University and Moore College. Their time in Australia reminded Arthur of his father's extended visit in 1892 which had helped kick-start CMS in that country. As he wrote: "If the extent of the sacrifice may be judged by the success, it must have been great."³⁷

大屠殺中倖存的孩子們

A few months later, on Tuesday 12 July, Kathleen and Ernest were married at St John's Cathedral, surrounded by an honor guard of students from both of their schools. After their honeymoon, they moved into SSC, where Ernest was acting Warden during the Headmaster's absence on sick leave. At this time there were sixty boarders, and one hundred and twenty day-boys from a range of Chinese provinces, including two sons of the Premier in Peking, and boys from rich Chinese communities in Australia, Indonesia, Malaysia, and Singapore. The staff consisted mainly of Chinese graduates from Oxford and Cambridge, as well as Hong Kong University. As Ernest wrote:

34. *Church Missionary Gleaner*, 2 February 1920, ch.1
35. Wolfendale, *History of St John's*, 122.
36. South China Mission Original Papers 1920–1922, 3 January 1922.
37. A. Stewart, After Seventy Years, 8.

> Life at St Stephen's is like that of all Public Schools. The boys used to sit for the local Oxford Examinations, but now they take the Matriculation Examination of Hong Kong University. Many Old Boys proceed to America or England for study . . . The School Association has a list of 1500 old members of the College, and it embraces names well known in China in official, business, and social circles. Many other Old Boys are working in humble spheres, doing quiet constructive work for their great country, endeavouring with success to practice those ideals which they learnt at their old school. The number of Christians among the Old Boys is now large.[38]

With enrolment of boarders exceeding accommodation, Kathleen threw herself into organizing extra beds, some even on the Martin's verandah. As Form III Mistress, there were over forty boys in her charge. She also added a 'feminine touch' to staff rooms and made their dining room more hospitable. Ernest often drew her into conversations with alumnae in their drawing-room where her fluency in Chinese shone.

Two significant events occurred during Kathleen's first year at St Stephen's. In January 1922 low-paid Chinese sailors went on strike when they could not obtain a wage rise. When port workers, also seeking a pay adjustment, came out in protest, food piled up on the wharves, and garbage went uncollected. Soon a hundred and twenty thousand other workers across the city—including clerks, waiters, tram conductors, and domestic servants—joined them. Half of these were either pressured or enticed to emigrate to Canton where they were promised a house, food, and a wage. Armed members of the Seamen's Union enforced the strike and blockaded all food by sea or rail. Toward the end of February, this crippling of the city led the Hong Kong government to bring in 'scab labor' from China. In reaction bakers, cooks, clerks, cleaners, and servants, joined the protest. The strike was only brought to an end through the arrest of its leaders, the army taking over food supplies and transport, and a prohibition against residents leaving the Colony even for weddings and funerals.[39] As SSC relied on various kinds of domestic workers to keep running, it was greatly affected by the strike. To overcome this, Kathleen helped students organize committees to do the work, and rose before five each morning to assist with cooking for students and staff.[40]

38. *The Outpost*, 1922, 6.

39. The post-War story of Hong Kong, including this event, is told by Carroll, *Concise History of Hong Kong*, 89–115, 5.

40. *The Chimes*, 36, 2, 1947, 8.

On 6 and 7 April, the Prince of Wales, later King Edward VIII, made an official two-day visit to Hong Kong.

> The majority of the population were [involved on] Friday in trying to follow him as he fulfilled a long programme of engagements. They gave him a rousing reception everywhere. The Prince began the day by meeting the students from 40 schools, Chinese scouts, guides, and nurses. He inspected the Indian 102nd Grenadiers, then laid the foundation stone of St Stephen's Girls College.[41]

Kathleen and Ernest were present at this important occasion marking the construction of new premises for the school. After this, the Prince went on to the University of Hong Kong, the races at Happy Valley, and a Chinese Banquet followed by a Ball.

The following year, the Martins left for study-leave to the UK. As well as meeting each other's families for the first time, they undertook the Teachers' Training Course in a newly created education department at Oxford University. They found rented accommodation in one of the large Victorian villas in north Oxford, not far from university parkland and the river Cherwell. Together they explored the many historic and cultural treasures of the city and took advantage of its proximity to London. The year gave them the opportunity to talk about what was important to them in education, especially as Ernest was likely to become St Stephen's next Headmaster. At the end of the course, Kathleen was honored by being elected to the Committee of the Oxford University Teachers' Association.

大屠殺中倖存的孩子們

Just before Christmas 1922, Arthur and Kitty arrived back in Hong Kong. The following year was a stressful one. Kitty was suffering from morning sickness and anxiety about the upcoming birth of their fourth child. As well as resuming his workload at the College, Arthur was also drawn into dealing with urgent issues on various CMS committees that consumed much of his time. After months of anticipation, on 14 August a healthy son, Arthur James Lander, was born. Though, over the next few months, he continued to thrive, Kitty began to develop symptoms of malaria. These became so debilitating that the CMS doctor recommended 'special leave' be granted to the Stewarts for the summer of 1924. Their plan was to spend that time in

---

41. *Australasian*, 15 April 1922, 38.

complete rest with her parents at their Vicarage in New Barnet, London. The only exception was to visit a now ailing aunt Tem in Dublin and see at first hand the memorial plaque honoring James in Monkstown Parish Church. Located behind the pulpit, this read:

> IN MEMORY OF
> REV. JAMES ROBERT STEWART, B.A.
> REPRESENTATIVE OF THIS PARISH IN W. CHINA
> TEMPORARY CHAPLAIN TO THE FORCES
> KILLED IN ACTION AT CAMBRIN, FRANCE.
> JAN. 2nd 1916 AGED 35 YEARS.
>
> "GREATER LOVE HATH NO MAN THAN THIS, THAT
> A MAN LAY DOWN HIS LIFE FOR HIS FRIENDS"
>
> ERECTED BY HIS FELLOW CHAPLAINS

Before they left, Arthur made his 15th Annual Report to the College, which emphasized 'further advances' that had been made. In this, he highlighted attendances being the highest on record; good results in the Local Examinations, and pleasing work being done in all Sections, especially the Junior Division; winning the Challenge Shield for athletics that was presented by Governor; extension of the College Chapel; erection of the Wu Ting Fang Hall to seat the whole school; senior students running a Free School at Causeway Bay and a Free Night School in the Hostel; staff and students giving a month each summer to teach street children to read. He concluded that if our teachers:

> ... thought that in this school we were equipping boys only for money making and world success we should have small satisfaction in the work, but each evidence of a willingness ... to serve others, gives an added impetus ... to press forward to the ideal we have set before ourselves in our school song, "to send from these walls a noble band who will work for the good of their country.[42]

"While Arthur was away, his brother was appointed acting Principal of the College. Evan was aware that, because of his interrupted studies at TCD, he lacked any official teaching qualifications. As London University would allow him to study externally, he decided to complete his degree in History. At this time, Evan also made an effort to improve his rudimentary Cantonese. Kathleen was by now a fluent speaker, and Arthur a little less so, but Evan found some of the complicated grammar and tones of the language

---

42. 'Annual Report 1923–1924' in A. Stewart, Annual Letters, 1923–24.

difficult.⁴³ He wanted to do better than most expats in the Colony, where "very few of the British, even after thirty years in the Colony, spoke more than a few words of Cantonese, most [being] limited to communicating with servants and rickshaw pullers in the horrors of pidgin English."⁴⁴

In Spring 1920, on reaching Szechwan the Taylors were assigned to the district of Chongkiang, where Mildred had worked before their marriage. This was around two days walk from Chengtu. As it was situated on the plain, for most of the year the climate was very humid and taxing. Along with the majority Sichuanese population, there were several ethnic minorities, including a few Tibetans. Pioneer missionary work was less than ten years old, and so far had received very little response. A CMS missionary couple and teacher had gone three years earlier, leaving no one to continue the work. By the time the Taylors arrived at their base in the town of Tungchwan, the church consisted of only one man and a handful of women. Apart from occasional visits by their friend Dr Lechler, they were the only Europeans for many miles around. Much of Reg's work was itinerant, often leaving Mil and their two young children for weeks at a time. Taking on this challenge fitted their approach to serving God, which was to try and "find the toughest places."⁴⁵ With Reg often itinerating for a few weeks at a time, they decided that the best way to handle their new situation was to find someone to assist Mildred in the home and in the work. Through Mil's friendship with Gladys Donnithorne, a fellow CMS missionary in the next district, she heard that Nellie Riley, a trained volunteer Quaker missionary had just arrived from England and was seeking a place to serve. The Taylors contacted her to ask ask if she would act as a nanny and assist Mildred in work amongst women.⁴⁶

A major part of Reg's work in the Chongkiang district involved regular preaching trips to unreached villages. Due to the risk of bandit groups in the area, traveling could be problematic. These were largely comprised of rural hoodlums, petty criminals, unpaid or demobilized soldiers. Villagers and townspeople, especially those on the road, regularly suffered most at their hands. Bandits sometimes kidnapped local people, including children, demanding a ransom. While, generally, they did not prevent missionaries from moving around, occasionally they forbade them to preach or hand out literature. Not only bandits, but even military based in the district

43. From personal correspondence with Evan's son, Michael Stewart.
44. Snow, *The Fall of Hong Kong*, 4.
45. From personal correspondence with Mildred's niece, Joan Mosley, 3 July 2020.
46. Nellie later went on to found an orphanage for Chinese children in Tungliang, West China.

sometimes acted against the law. Soldiers pressured farmers to grow opium for their own profit, and also extorted protection money from villagers, torturing them if they refused to comply.

Mildred's approach to reaching women mostly involved home visits, assisted by one of the local female Christians. While this was a slow process, these women who were unused to talking about anything but domestic matters, gradually began to respond. Each day Mildred also preached in the centrally located Women's Guest Hall. This large building, open to the street much like a modern 'drop-in' center, provided a place to socialize and offered free meals to women passing by. Thirty or forty locals would regularly gather to hear a 'foreign devil' speak in their dialect about her strange philosophy. Alongside this, Mildred supervised Bible-woman who worked mostly in surrounding villages, gaining the interest of wives whose husbands allowed them to attend classes on Christianity.

When Reg was in Tungchwan, he also spoke daily in the Men's Guest Hall, with his assistant, Mr Ton, a Chinese evangelist, taking his place during his absences. Since there was no hospital in the vicinity, opium addicts sometimes came into town seeking help from him at the Guest Hall. During their first year, Reg set up a recovery program through which a number of these, including two Tibetan priests, were freed from the habit. The small church in the town gradually began to grow, with a noticeable increase in men showing interest.

In 1922, a new assistant Bishop from the UK was installed in West Szechwan. It was the first episcopal appointment since the War, which most assumed would have gone to James but for his death. The Taylors had heard about Howard Mowll through mutual connections at both Cambridge University and Ridley Hall. They appreciated his encouragement during tours of the Diocese and were pleased when they heard about his engagement to Dorothy Martin, a fellow CMS missionary in Szechwan. Having been born in Foochow, where her parents had worked with Robert and Louisa Stewart, Dorothy had taught at the same school as Mildred in Mienchuh. They looked forward to attending their wedding and to spending time with both of them on future pastoral visits.

Unfortunately, Reg's health issues began to resurface, reducing his capacity to do itinerant ministry. Coupled with this, there was a rapid decay in law and order throughout the whole district, with bandit raids and military reprisals a frequent occurrence. The constant fighting during 1923 prevented a new missionary, Mr Philips, from joining them, as well as Dr Lechler from checking on them. The worst incident occurred in August, when two of their colleagues from Mienchow, Revs Watt and Whiteside, were on a sightseeing trip in the mountains. During the summer, guided by several locals, they were taking the opportunity to collect and photograph specimens for their Boys School museum. "Suddenly at about 11 o'clock a volley of rifle shots rang out, startling the Chinese who ducked and ran for cover . . . After the firing had ceased and the shouting had quietened down, they came out of hiding . . . Running back along the road they found [the two missionaries] dead, each wounded in several places . . . and lying on the road where they had fallen", their possessions having all been taken.[47] This news shocked the whole mission and, as Reg wrote, "paralysed all our energies."[48] For Mildred, this violence brought back painful memories and increased fears for their young children.

The following year she also fell ill and, for most of 1924, the Taylors were only able to take on half their usual workload. As their health deteriorated, the Mission ordered them to take an extended sick leave in Shanghai.

---

47. *West China Missionary News*, September 1923, 6 (see also 7–9. 29–31) and for the memorial later set up in their honor, *West China Missionary News*, May 1924, 1–2.

48. R. Taylor, Annual Letter 1923–24, 1.

5

Living Through Troubled Times (1925–1938)

ON 30 MAY 1925, police under British command in Shanghai's International Settlement fired into a large crowd of Chinese demonstrators who were protesting against their workplace conditions. Nine people were killed and many others were wounded. News of the event spread quickly to other major cities in China, especially Canton where a similar incident occurred in the British Concession on Shamin Island. Until two months earlier, Sun Yat-sen had been the commanding figure in the Kuomintang Coalition Government based in Canton but, with his death from cancer in March, leadership had been aggressively taken over by the head of the Communist Party. Under the latter's influence, the Kuomintang clamored for a general strike in neighboring Hong Kong, offering free transport, accommodation, and jobs for all Chinese willing to move to Canton.

In Hong Kong, this strike proved to be "the most significant event of the inter-War period."[1]

In early June, Communist agitators from Canton were sent to Hong Kong to stir up university students there to call employees in several key occupations to stop work. Though working conditions in the Colony were fairly good in comparison to mainland China, unions demanded a general strike for an eight-hour workday, reductions in rent, and a Chinese representative on the Legislative Council.

Over the next few weeks, strike leaders put pressure on Hong Kong's government by placing a partial embargo on goods leaving the Colony.

---

1. Carroll, *Concise History of Hong Kong*, 99.

Living Through Troubled Times (1925–1938) 97

More than two hundred thousand workers also took up the Canton Government's offer to move there. This led to a significant shut down of Hong Kong, with only token public transport operating, hospitals threatening closure, extended water shortages, and a looming financial crisis. Virtually all domestic helpers, janitorial services, and sanitation workers, downed tools in the city.[2]

In September, at the start of the new academic year, with less public transport and picketing of teachers, schools suffered lower attendance and disruption. At SSC, where Ernest was now Deputy Warden and Kathleen Form III Mistress: "The School was influenced by secret agitators in May and June, but the anti-foreign and anti-religious propaganda and spirit were evident in Hong Kong for five months before the Shanghai and Canton incidents... In spite of agitators both within and without the School, our boys remained loyal and did not 'strike.'"[3]

Hong Kong in the mid-1920s

Since Arthur was known to have a broad interest in the affairs of the Colony, he was asked to become the Official Chaplain to the Forces, and also join the Hong Kong Board of Education. His response to the strike reflects this:

2. For more detail see Carroll, *Edge of Empires,* 131–148 and Horrocks, The Guangzhou-Hongkong Strike.

3. E. Martin, Annual Letter, October 1925, 1.

The two shootings at Shanghai and Shamin, were most unfortunate, ... They give a fine scope for anti-British propaganda, and a good foundation for lies, of the most amazing kind. So much so that a girl in a Hong Kong CMS School, for many years in the Colony, feared to travel in a British steamer for she knew she would be murdered! The passive attitude adopted since then, objected to by the bitter spirits out here, has undoubtedly taken the wind out of the enemies' sails, and is bringing things gradually back to normal, particularly here in Hong Kong. All our schools opened here in September, but with very many depleted numbers, owing to the activities of the strike pickets. St Paul's College began with 16 boarders instead of 70, and 250 day-boys instead of over 500. Gradually they have been coming back in all sorts of interesting ways. Some have gone all the way to Shanghai and back again here, some have shipped as sailors on junks, two dressed as bare-footed beggars and walked for days, and so slipped through. It amuses us to see their delight at getting back to Hong Kong and we only wish that the Canton Authorities could see this evidence of flattery for the 'imperialists'!

It is evident to all that the boycott could have collapsed long ago but for the double feat of Soviet support and money from Russia, and the vast sums obtained by the strike leaders by squeezing vessels to pay as much as $1000 for permission to land cargo. It is not to be expected that these men could care that the whole commercial life of South China is faced with ruin.

I must confess I rather dreaded the opening of school not knowing what to expect and knowing that absurd and false things had been written about one in the Chinese papers. One account said that on a patriotic occasion when the boys were carrying the flag of China, I seized the flag, trod it under foot and beat the boys! ... A real effort is being made to undermine our schools and bring them into bad odour

[Regarding St Paul's Church] ... at first, of course, there was a sort of electric feeling in the air and so many lies were being told, that some of our people were carried away and some said foolish things, but the pendulum soon swung back again and all was well between us. I shall always remember with a happy feeling the service in St Paul's Church on the first Sunday in August ... the sense of such real devotion and worship, that we were one in Christ, whatever unhappy divisions there may be outside.

[Overall] we can certainly see good coming out of it all. China certainly has grievances and foreigners have not been as sympathetic as they might have been about them. We have every hope now that there will be better mutual understanding after this, and one can already see that the Chinese are going to be given greater responsibilities and wider scope for self-expression ... for which in many cases they are quite prepared.[4]

For the Stewart family, 1925 was a year of mixed blessings. Back in Dublin, aunt Tem had "passed quietly away, having devoted practically her whole life to making a home for us. One result was that Brighton Lodge ceased to be our home."[5] Unable to attend the funeral, Arthur, Kathleen, and Evan got together to share their memories of her over the past thirty years. A happy event was the birth of Arthur and Kitty's first daughter, Margaret. Another celebration was Evan's graduating from London University and TCD's recognition of this, conferring on him the 'right to wear the cap and gown of a graduate'.

Mildred and family in England

4. A. Stewart, Annual Letter, November 1925, 1–4.
5. A. Stewart, After Seventy Years, 16.

In February 1926, with a long-planned Chapel and physics laboratory completed, and fewer students enrolled in the College, CMS granted Arthur and Kitty special leave to stay with the Landers in London. From there they were also able to spend time with the Taylors in Tunbridge Wells where Reg was now working as a part-time Curate. Mildred had ultimately been diagnosed with phlebitis, a serious venous inflammation in her damaged leg, which regularly caused burning sensation like hot needles along the vein. Though she was able to do some household chores, and make short trips outside their home, on bad days it was difficult for her to remain standing for any length of time. In its most serious form, blood clots could develop and potentially travel to the lungs. Before the use of blood-thinning drugs, the only ways of reducing pain and minimizing further damage were rest in bed, elevating the leg, application of heat, and use of compression stockings. Since this was a chronic condition, CMS reluctantly decided that their return to China was out of the question. As she had always seen her call to China as a life-long commitment, Mildred took this very hard. It was some time before she fully came to terms with the fact that God was now leading them as a family in a different direction.

大屠殺中倖存的孩子們

Back in Hong Kong, Ernest and Kathleen were in the middle of protracted negotiations about relocating St Stephen's. With the lease on the original property running out, some classes and activities had already moved into temporary accommodation while a new property was being sought. The Hong Kong government had provided a site of twenty-five acres on the Stanley Peninsula in the south of the island, and the decision was made to transfer there as soon as funding was available for the buildings. Part of their considerable cost would be covered by a government grant, part by a government loan to be repaid by CMS over ten years, with the rest having to be raised by an appeal to Old Boys of the College.

Along with teaching, Kathleen threw herself into the task of organizing events in aid of the new building fund. One of these, a three-day fundraising bazaar held in the Great Hall of the University, had concluded at the same hour the strike in Hong Kong began! She was the guiding spirit in the staging of plays and concerts, sometimes taking part herself. Her 'beautiful voice' was appreciated and long-remembered by students at St. Stephen's.[6] "In several of these efforts Mrs Martin was the leading figure, and her

---

6. *The Chimes*, 36. 2, 1947, 7.

cheerfulness and happiness inspired staff and students."⁷ As Ernest wrote: "My wife has been the only lady at the School during the year, and her work as a Form Mistress, and a Caterer, and in every possible way, is invaluable."⁸ Unfortunately, all this took its toll and eventually Kathleen was admitted to hospital suffering from overwork and stress.

As the strike rolled on into 1926, all sea trade along the South China coast was placed in Chinese hands, and policed by 20,000 uniformed pickets patrolling rivers and other strategic locations. In February, trains to and from the mainland were blocked, and shots were fired on police launches and British Army soldiers in the New Settlements. The Colonial Government declared a state of emergency, imposed a curfew, and mobilized volunteers to guard streets and fill empty jobs. Unlike the agitators from Canton, unions in Hong Kong accepted the benefits of the British presence and sought incremental rather than radical changes in their working conditions. Unions also increasingly resented attempts by representatives from Canton to take them over. For these reasons, mass support for the strike gradually ebbed, particularly as the trade boycott severely affected people's everyday lives in the Colony. Hong Kong authorities also realized the need to work more closely with leaders of the Chinese community. In May, the Governor appointed the first Chinese member of the Executive Council and required University lecturers to place more emphasis on Chinese culture and morality.

Ernest, who that year was acting-Warden at St John's Hall as well as Deputy Headmaster at St Stephen's, captures the mood of the College:

> Our feeling is one of thankfulness and wonder for have we not also weathered all the political anniversary days of May and June without the slightest trouble or disturbance? . . . The feeling of the School this year has been friendly to foreigners and sympathetic to Christianity . . . we in Hong Kong have been privileged to carry on our work undisturbed when so many institutions all over China have been closed. There are signs that Chinese students are coming in increasing numbers to Hong Kong because of the peace it offers for study, and that Chinese parents are sending their sons to Hong Kong more than ever for security while China is making her great struggle for unification. One wonders whether Hong Kong is not to be *one* of the strategic points for missionary work during the next 20 years?⁹

7. *The Chimes*, 36. 2, 1947, 9.
8. E. Martin, Annual Letter, October 1925, 2.
9. E. Martin, Annual Letter, November 1927, 2–4. See also the reports in *The Hong Kong Telegraph*, 24 June 1927, 8 and in the *Church Missionary Outlook*, December

It was only in October that the strike came to an end, and a degree of normality returned to the Colony.

大屠殺中倖存的孩子們

In the only letter she wrote to CMS, Kathleen opened her heart about the pressures of unrealistic demands on missionaries that had long been present but which the strike had amplified.

> I feel stirred up to my very depth as I heard by last mail of many offering as missionaries after the last Keswick, and by nearly the last mail that home folk seem to feel China almost an impossible field just now, yet to us here . . . the opportunities are immense. The Chinese are asking for our friendship and co-operation, and the workers grow fewer every year . . . The tragedy is that the shortage is throwing on to those who are left such a weight of the business side of things, that cannot honourably be left out, that the time for sharing friendships . . . is of necessity squeezed out . . . [The last half year] was probably the hardest six months I have personally known, hard because we knew we were neglecting utterly the real work, hard because one's body felt often too tired to carry on, too tired to be friendly when students wanted to stay late talking, yet that is what we feel is needed in China now more than ever before . . . Friendships can do such wonders towards leading them to know and love Jesus Christ, but friendships take time . . . Chinese have said openly in meetings that missionaries do not care about them, they have told me this in private also. They want us as their friends, and we who love them so dearly have so little time in which to give . . . It is true that Chinese [Christian] workers are increasing in numbers, but not nearly fast enough for the opportunities, and even then, here at least, they like the foreigner to help as a friend . . . Therefore we do long that people at home realise this, and thrust out missionaries into China. Hong Kong's needs are *urgent* and there is no hindrance here to Christian work . . . among this most lovable people.[10]

On 27 April 1928, the foundation stone for St Stephen's was laid in Stanley by Sir Cecil Clementi, the Governor of Hong Kong, along with official guests representing both the church and Colony. Evan was also present,

---

1927, 257.

10. K. Martin, Annual Letter, 3 September 1927, 1–4.

having ridden down on his newly purchased motorcycle. In his address, the Governor said that the occasion " . . . marked the beginning of a new era in educational enterprise in the Colony, in that they were attempting no less than to found here a Public School after the model of those in the United Kingdom . . . an institution not only with a high standard of education but of public service for the good of others."[11] It was, in fact, the first time the College would have a building of its own, with ample space for playing grounds, and for future expansion. As its magazine noted: "Much of the planning of buildings and their details was due to Mrs Martin's woman's mind. Almost every day in the Summer of 1928, she travelled in Mr Martin's side-car to Stanley to see the buildings in construction, afterwards having tea in a matshed [a small marquee made out of matting] on the school beach."[12] After the Governor had laid the foundation stone, he was presented with a scroll of Chinese poems composed by students in honor of the occasion, and with a silver trowel and blackwood mallet by the Building Committee. A dedicatory prayer brought the ceremony to a close, after which the gathering sat down for tea and refreshments.

Originally one of the oldest fishing villages, Stanley was a coastal town around twelve miles by road from downtown Hong Kong. It had been an early place of British settlement and the first administrative center in the Colony. At this time, there was an historic temple, a police station, and a small military barracks, to protect that end of the island. Building commenced immediately on an assembly hall, classrooms and dormitory, and would take an estimated two years to complete.

Around this time, the Stewarts in Hong Kong had an unexpected visitor. The previous year, Philip had been transferred to China with the Shanghai Defence Corps. This detachment was mobilised after British residents in Hankow had to take refuge in a cruiser on the Yangtze while Nationalist troops were fighting to restore the Republic. Fearing that the International Settlement in Shanghai was at risk, the contingent was formed out of sixteen military units in the British army.[13] One of these was Philip's regiment in Malta.

On arrival, the sixteen thousand strong force was quartered at the Shanghai Racecourse, though Philip was based at the Military Hospital

11. *The Hong Kong Telegraph*, 28 April 1928, 2.

12. *The Chimes*, 36. 2, 1947, 9.

13. In the House of Commons, support for this was advocated on the ground of protecting British lives and property, and arguments against it raised by those concerned it would have a negative influence on missionary work. In the end, by a vote of 241 to 116, the motion was approved. See HC Deb 16 March 1927 vol 203 cc2112–63. At api.parliament.uk › historic-hansard › commons › mar.

near the Bund. Its purpose was to create and patrol a twelve-mile cordon around the International Settlement, which was occasionally sniped at from surrounding buildings. Since injuries were few, however, Philip's work consisted mainly of treating soldiers for various tropical diseases. By the end of the year, tensions began to ease, particularly after Chiang Kai Shek's victory and violent purge of Communists in the city. As the number of British troops was gradually reduced, Philip was able to visit Hong Kong, partly because the Defence Force's Base Hospital was located there. He stayed with Arthur and Kitty, enjoyed going down to Stanley with Ernest and Kathleen to see the progress of St Stephen's, and was introduced by Evan to officers in the HKVDC. This visit raised the possibility in Philip's mind of returning to Hong Kong in a few years when his military service concluded.

When, early in 1929, the Malta regiment was finally withdrawn from Shanghai, Philip took six months accumulated leave in Ireland. While there, through his military connections, he met Nina Brownlow. Fifteen years younger than Philip, Nina came from Portaferry, near Belfast. Her family's estate, Ballywhite House, was a stately home on a wooded five-hundred-acre property. Guy, her eldest brother, had been a decorated Colonel in WW1 and, Gwendoline, her eldest sister, had served as a Matron in various overseas military hospitals.[14] It was probably through her that Philip was introduced to Nina, and he spent much of his leave courting her. After three months back with his regiment in Malta, Philip took a further brief leave, and on 5 November he and Nina married in Ballyphilip Parish Church.

In Hong Kong, Evan had also become romantically involved. He had known Dorothy, the younger daughter of Bishop Lander, since their boarding school days in England. The boys of Wellington College and girls from Sherborne Girls School occasionally had combined social events. It was during one of these that the two met briefly at a skating rink in London. "He pulled her pig-tails and they did not like each other at all!"[15] After Sherborne, Dorothy returned to Hong Kong, first working for a company in the city, and then training as a nurse at the Matilda Hospital. As well as seeing her at Cathedral services each week, after Arthur married her older sister, Kitty, Evan and Dorothy were often both present at family get-togethers. They also met regularly in the active social life of Hong Kong, such as informal 'tiffins', beach parties, sporting fixtures, concerts, and plays. "Evan and Dorothy clearly enjoyed each other's company." [16]

14. See 'William Claude Barabizon Brownlow', The Peerage. At https://www.thepeerage.com.

15. This detail was provided by Michael Stewart in personal correspondence.

16. These remarks are largely drawn from personal correspondence with their son, Michael Stewart.

Living Through Troubled Times (1925–1938)

Evan and Dorothy's wedding

In July 1927 they announced their engagement and six months later, on 25 January 1928, were married by Arthur at St John's Cathedral. They moved into a large, comfortable flat on the top floor of a building on Bowen Rd, overlooking Victoria Harbour and the distant Kowloon Hills. In addition to his College responsibilities, Evan had now offered to help lead the 10th Hong Kong Scout Group that met on its campus, partly because many of its members went on to join the HKVDC.[17] As for some time he had been the assistant Headmaster at the College, Arthur talked with Evan about his desire to hand over its leadership at his next furlough in a couple of years. Not long before he had asked his Chinese colleague, Rev Paul T'so to become Vicar of St Paul's Church.

大屠殺中倖存的孩子們

In the middle of 1929, after much effort by the Martins and their staff, the relocation of SSC was completed. Shortly afterwards, Ernest wrote:

17. Fung, *From Devotion to Plurality*, 220–221. An overview of the Scout Group's history at SPC is provided on 220–224.

This is a historic spot, having been occupied by the British garrison of the colony some eighty years ago. It is a magnificent peninsula, jutting out into the Pacific Ocean and swept by all the prevailing summer winds. The old military parade ground is now converted into playing fields where Chinese boys play football, cricket, basket-ball, and other games. Eight tennis courts are being constructed, and swimming is taught in delightful sandy bays immediately below the school. The main building, occupied in May last, contains the School Hall, and twelve large classrooms, with accommodation on the upper floor for boarders and staff. Ample servants' quarters have been provided, and electric light, telephone, garage, a first-rate water supply, and so far two bungalows for married masters. A second large building is on the point of being completed. This includes additional accommodation for boarders and staff with common rooms for both; and a fine communal dining hall, with kitchens.

Over twenty-five years St Stephen's College has been a town school with about 150 boys, of whom some 50 were boarders. Now it has moved to a spacious site in the country, with superb scenery on all sides, accommodation has been provided for 100 boarders, and it is hoped to develop this side of the school much farther. The whole site has been carefully planned by a competent architect, so that chapel, sanitorium, libraries, laboratories, and additional boarding houses may be erected as finances permit. The central and highest part of the isthmus has been reserved for the chapel, which will cost 5000 pounds, and will be a church for the south side of the island and a striking landmark not only from the Peak but far out at sea for ships approaching Hong Kong and China. School prayers are alternatively in Chinese and English, that is, on three days in one language and three days in the other. The reason for this is that all the boys learn English, for the purposes of university education, commerce, or travel; and many Chinese boys come from overseas to learn Chinese, so that English for them is often the language they know best ... Mention may be made of a free night school for poor boys which has been carried on by our students for the past four years with discipline and success.[18]

Ernest went on to talk about the academic achievements of the College. Many boys were now studying at Hong Kong University, and sixteen were undertaking postgraduate work in England, America, and elsewhere overseas. Several graduates occupied important offices in the National

---

18. E. Martin, *Church Missionary Outlook*, November 1929, 227–229.

Government. A handful had refused lucrative positions to teach in the College. Others were serving in Churches or in Mission hospitals on the Mainland. Many were also working in commerce and the professions. Present students include "a large number of non-Christian boys drawn from the official, commercial, professional and other leading classes, both from China itself and Chinese communities overseas." [19]

For Kathleen's work:

> A new feature was the number of small boys. These were housed in five rooms adjoining the Warden's bedroom. In acting as Mother to these boys, and to all the boarders, Mrs. Martin attained a height of service and efficiency. She had mothered forty boarders, now she had one hundred and sixty. Her care of young boys and sick boys was whole-hearted, amounting to devotion, and her skill equalled to that of a highly trained nurse. She continued to teach Geography and her students attained distinctions in the Hong Kong University Matriculation Examination. From the first she had taken an enthusiastic interest in school sports, spending many an afternoon watching football matches or athletic contests. She taught many students their first tennis, numbers of students to swim, and delighted to join in the swimming parties at Stanley.[20]

That same year, Arthur and Kitty announced the birth of Joan, their second daughter. Not long after, believing that his pioneering contribution to St Paul's was complete, Arthur stepped down and officially handed over leadership to Evan. Both felt that it was good for him to stay on for a while, so that his "going caused no upheaval" [21] or loss of confidence among supporters.[22] The public announcement of Arthur's handing the baton to "his good Lieutenant" took place on 15 March 1930 as part of the 80th Anniversary Celebration of the College, which was held at the Theatre Royal in the city. The event was headline news, and spread over four pages, in the Hong Kong Sunday Herald. Under the title 'Educational Progress: St Paul's Unique History', it reported that the venue was thronged with well-wishers and parents of students. On the platform were His Excellency, Hon W. T. Southorn C.M.G., the Government Administrator; Rt Rev Dr C. R. Duppuy,

---

19. E. Martin, *Church Missionary Outlook*, November 1929, 229.
20. *The Chimes*, 36. 2, 1947, 9–10.
21. For this description see *The Hong Kong Daily Press*, 19 July 1930, 7.
22. A. Stewart, After Seventy Years, 16.

the Bishop of Victoria; Sir Henry Pollack K.C.; the Hon Dr S. W. T'so; Mr E. Ralphs, Director of Education and Rev Paul T'so, Vicar of St Paul's Church.[23]

After a speech by the Bishop—which mentioned that "everyone knew Arthur Stewart, and he knew almost everyone", and that he was welcome at Government House as warmly as at . . . St Paul's and other Chinese Churches"[24]—Arthur rose to speak:

> For personal reasons, today is of peculiar interest to myself as it represents the completion of 21 years as headmaster of St Paul's College. It has often been in my mind that the day must come when I shall have been long enough in my present position and shall feel it right to hand it over to another. This occasion seems eminently fitting for such action as so today for the last time I read the annual report and for the last time take my place as headmaster. Not that I mean that I am deserting the old ship; rather let me put it this way, that, having walked the bridge for 21 years with all the responsibilities and anxieties that such a post involves, I am now reversing the usual order of things and retiring to the foc'sle to become one of the 'hands' before the mast.
>
> This is an easy thing to do when I know that the wheel will be in such capable hands as those of my brother, who has already been on the staff for 17 years, with the backing and support of as loyal a staff as any headmaster could desire. I have tried each year, in vain, to express what can never be put into adequate words, the sense of deep indebtedness to the faithful, willing service of all members of the staff. Teachers may come and teachers may go, but the same spirit remains, a spirit of willingness to help, and of love for the school they serve. [25]

Arthur first recounted the early 'start-stop' attempts of St Paul's from 1850 to 1908. Then he outlined the progress of the present 'reconstituted' school, including the establishment of three branch schools in Aberdeen, Causeway Bay and Kowloon.

> During these past 21 years nearly 4000 boys have passed through the school and are to be found in all parts of the world . . . It is hardly an exaggeration to say that one cannot enter any office, bank or business establishment in this Colony without a look of recognition and smile of welcome from some 'Old Boy'. Many have already made their mark in the world. I mention just

23. *Hong Kong Sunday Herald*, 16 March 1930, 1, 8, 13, 18.
24. *Wayfarer*, 1, 1957–1958, 48.
25. *Wayfarer*, 1, 1957–1958, 52–53.

at random the head of a large firm in Shanghai, the manager of a bank in Canton, seven who are now in the medical profession; of last year's graduates from the Hong Kong University four were 'Old Boys'. In educational work we have a headmaster of a school in Canton, another in Shanghai, and an Inspector of Schools in Singapore. Of the staff in our school eleven are 'Old Boys', and others are teachers in different parts of the world, including Church Schools in Borneo and far off New Zealand . . . Already eight of our 'Old Boys' have entered Theological Colleges to read for Holy Orders and we are expecting that others will soon follow in their steps. A school song composed in our early days sums up our ideal in the words: 'We'll send from these walls a noble band, who will work for the good of their country.'[26]

In conclusion, Hon R. W. Southorn congratulated Arthur on his unique contribution to the College, commending him in the following words: "We can but admire the courage and self-sacrifice that have inspired the Headmaster to lay down the reins of office and accept a humble position in the dominion over which he has ruled . . . his example should be an inspiration to service to past, present and future boys of St Paul's College."[27]

Arthur, Kitty and the children then left for furlough in England, staying with the Landers at New Barnet in London. Once again, they were able to spend time with Reg and Mil, who were now serving at St George's Church, the Weald, in Kent.

大屠殺中倖存的孩子們

Evan became Principal at the age of thirty-eight. Though grateful for all that Arthur had done to establish the College, Evan now had the opportunity to put his stamp on SPC. Having been on the staff already for many years—as a teacher, sports-master, and then Deputy Principal—he saw getting to know students as individuals as a high priority. During morning and lunch breaks, and after school, instead of going to his office, he was often found chatting with students or kicking a ball with them in the grounds. Many photos show him relaxed and enjoying their company. This attitude developed a College

---

26. *Wayfarer*, 1, 1957–1958, 53.
27. *Hong Kong Sunday Herald*, 16 March 1930, 18.

culture in which "relationships between students and the staff was indeed very close, unlike most schools at the time."[28]

Evan also believed that SPC's Christian group, the YMCA, had an active role to play in the life of the College. Run by students, this organised:

> a quarter of an hour's service every morning. Every Saturday morning, at 9am, there was morning prayer in the chapel, with sermons given by famous speakers or staff members. There were a considerable number of students interested in the Bible, hence a Bible class was inaugurated and was very well attended throughout the year. There was a Baptism Class for those students who were ready to be baptised. There was also a prayer meeting at 11am every Wednesday in the YMCA Office.
>
> [The YMCA also organised] . . .the Debating Club and the Library in the College. Outside the College, the YMCA was responsible for the Tai Hang Free School, including the appointment of teachers there. The Association also sent some of its members to preach open air every Monday evening . . . with an audience of no less than a hundred every time. Moreover . . . [at] St Mary's Church, they held a service or Sunday school, for the four neighbouring schools every Thursday at 3pm. More than a hundred students attended the service every time. Furthermore, the College YMCA joined the Hong Kong Student Association. Representatives were sent to attend seasonal conferences, which were held four times a year. There were also retreats, united students' prayer meetings, social meetings and picnics etc.[29]

As one would expect, Evan continued to encourage the value of sport in the College, particularly athletics which remained his special interest. In the following years, St Paul's continued to excel in local sporting competitions. Through his involvement on various education committees, he frequently enquired about the role of sports in other schools and sought to increase the number and range of inter-school competitions. He believed that competition between teams brought out the best in boys, which ultimately contributed to the quality of the schools and wider society.

Evan was also keen to develop SPC's relationship with its graduates. Though an alumni association had existed for some years, it was relatively dormant. When he became Principal, "over a hundred boys had a meeting with the Stewart brothers and all teaching staff. There was a prolonged discussion of starting an 'Old Pauline Union', and it was obvious at that meeting that the overwhelming majority, including the Stewart brothers, were in

---

28. Fung, *From Devotion to Plurality*, 63.
29. Fung, *From Devotion to Plurality*, 175–176.

favour of the idea." [30] A provisional President, and twenty-one committee members, were chosen. Though as yet the association had no formal name, because Evan and some staff maintained links with many recent alumni, it grew steadily. Before long, similar groups were set up in Canton and Shanghai.

Several months before Evan took over as Principal, Philip and Nina had arrived in Hong Kong from Malta. He was filling in at the British Military Hospital while the Senior Medical Officer was on a three-month leave. With a commanding view over Victoria Harbour, this had a maximum capacity of two hundred beds and was staffed by members of the RAMC. Since Philip was then due to retire, he would take up the newly created position of Medical Officer at SSC. With all the benefits of a full military pension, he and Nina wanted to serve in this way for several years. After introducing Nina to the wider family, they quickly settled into a flat in Pokfulam Rd, not far from Evan and Dorothy. So, finally, the last of the six Stewart children was involved in mission work in China!

Philip at St Stephen's College

30. Fung, *From Devotion to Plurality,* 233.

In December, Philip commenced at the College. Up to this point, Kathleen had acted as its 'unofficial' nurse and was relieved that Philip was now available, especially as malaria was a constant issue. Among his responsibilities were teaching classes on hygiene and nutrition; routine medical and dental check-ups; dealing with sporting and playground accidents; vaccination and monitoring for infectious diseases. Philip also set up a free medical clinic in Stanley Village for local people, especially fishermen and their families. A significant contribution he made during this time was to set up health protocols that eliminated transmission of malaria in the village.

With the Stewart family being so well-known and trusted in Hong Kong, early on Philip was asked to become a Medical Advisor to the Government. He and Nina were put on the official invitation list for dinner parties at Government House when distinguished visitors were passing through the Colony. As a Major in the British Army, he was always welcome at formal and informal events at the barracks, and often socialized in these circles. They also became part of the St John's Cathedral community.

In May 1931, Evan and Dorothy welcomed their son, Michael, who was born at the Matilda Hospital not far from where they were living. The whole Stewart clan took the opportunity to celebrate the happy occasion. Kathleen and Ernest talked about their upcoming plans to visit St Stephen's alumni in various parts of south-east Asia. Their purpose was two-fold: to see how their ex-students were faring and, through them, to raise the profile of the College. In the summer break, they set out for Penang, Singapore, Foochow, Amoy, Swatow, Macau, and Canton.[31] While in Foochow, they were able to visit Trinity College as well as the graves of Kathleen's parents.

In September that year, an unexpected event occurred in the region. Japan invaded Manchuria, the northernmost part of China, to gain access to natural resources necessary for its ongoing industrial development. This was in response to an embargo on Japan importing raw materials from the USA. The invasion was highly popular in Japan, as it was viewed as saving the country from the effects of the Depression. Though seen in Hong Kong as a sign of Japan's increasing imperial ambitions, it was not regarded as a potential threat to the Colony.

The following year, as Arthur and Kitty were considering where they should spend the final decade of their ministry and the long-term education of their children, a letter came from England. It offered Arthur the position of Vicar in the Parish of Holy Trinity, New Barnet in London. This vacancy had come about because Bishop Lander had been appointed as Archdeacon

---

31. E. Martin, *Annual Letter*, 21 June 1931, 1–2.

of Bedford.³² Though it was heart-breaking to leave Hong Kong, they felt this was the right step and accepted the offer.

In December, Arthur and Evan represented the College at the installation of Rev Ronald Owen Hall as the new Bishop of Hong Kong in St John's Cathedral. They welcomed the fact that he had distinguished himself in the War, already spent some time in China, acted as a mediator between the British and Chinese after the Shanghai incident, and was committed to an indigenous Church. Just before Arthur left for England, he received a public commendation in the *South China Morning Post*. A warm tribute was paid not only to what he had achieved but to the kind of person he was. "He is ever generous, warm-hearted, ingenious, far-seeing and imaginative, displaying a singularly lovable character and a remarkably indomitable spirit. To all who knew him, he has always been an object of admiration and envy, a man of courage and decision, with a vigorous mind and a blameless life."³³ Then, as Arthur wrote: "The closing days were filled with the usual speeches and farewell presentations and then on Sunday July 16, I preached to a very full St Paul's Church at 11am on 'The Love of God', went on board the *Conte Verde* and sailed. In less than four weeks I was instituted in the Parish. I don't think that anyone, least of all myself, realised how difficult it was, after 28 years of educational work, to take up the work of a Parish."³⁴

大屠殺中倖存的孩子們

Around this time, Hong Kong was belatedly beginning to feel some of the effects of the Great Depression which had been severely affecting the West for several years. Up till now, the Colony had been mostly protected from the stock market crash because its currency, like China's, was based on the silver standard, not the gold standard that had been so devalued in most other countries. By the end of 1933, however, with Hong Kong's reliance so much on international trade, the reduction of imports and exports was starting to impact its economy. This led to the fall of a large bank, increased unemployment, and ultimately a reduction in school enrolments. As donations to CMS worldwide were also decreasing, the South China Mission staff and institutions were now receiving less income.

---

32. A. Stewart, After Seventy Years, 16.

33. This was written by Colonel V. H. G. Jarett, a *South China Morning Post* columnist, and comes from private correspondence with Michael Stewart.

34. A. Stewart, After Seventy Years, 16–17.

New St Stephen's campus at Stanley

At St Paul's, "the depression... hit the School very heavily, and caused the overdraft to become considerable."[35] Despite this, however, an unexpected promise of a gift to the building fund made it possible to erect five long overdue classrooms. At St Stephen's, Ernest had a greater challenge. He had been warned that, if the College became unviable, the Government would appropriate its buildings for a prison it had just begun to build in Stanley. With the College for the first time facing debt, its Council approached key Chinese supporters for help; pleaded with CMS for special consideration; and asked staff whether, if necessary, they would be willing to take a modest pay-cut. Fortunately, almost enough money was raised, and the shortfall covered by temporarily withholding the CMS annual levy. This provision was sufficient to allow Ernest and Kathleen to go ahead with their much-needed furlough in the middle of 1934. Around the same time, Philip and Nina welcomed the arrival of their daughter, Mary Louisa, and decided it was time to set up their first real home, in Northern Ireland. At Philip's farewell from St Stephen's, at which locals from the village were also present, he was gratefully acknowledged as the one whose medical expertise "gave confidence and skill, and laid the foundation for the school's reputation for health."[36]

From her earliest days, Kathleen had a love for the natural world. As a teacher of Geography, her longing was to visit places she had only read about. One of these was Africa, with its scenic mountains, vast savannahs, exotic wildlife, and diverse cultures. So, the first leg of the Martins' furlough was Kenya, then a British Protectorate. After disembarking in the port

---

35. Mentioned in *South China Mission Education Committee*, CMS, 1937–1949, no page. See also the report in *The China Mail*, 10 February 1934, 1.

36. *The Chimes*, 36. 2, 1947, 6.

of Mombasa, they traveled by rail to the capital Nairobi. From there the Martins went on safari, the Swahili word for 'journey', to see up close lions, tigers, leopards, zebras and rhinoceroses, as well as snow-capped Mount Kenya. Through their CMS contacts, they were also able to visit several schools and churches in the country.

Moving on they sailed to Dar-es-Salaam in Tanzania, then to Durban and Capetown in South Africa, spending a few days in each, before heading to England. Arriving in Southampton, they travelled up to London, and stayed for a time with Arthur and Kitty in New Barnet.[37] The final leg of their furlough took them to New York. While there, "Kathleen fully entered into the enjoyment and excitement of Broadway and Times Square . . . it was her own capacity to enjoy which perhaps gave so much joy to others."[38] After this, they traveled by train to Niagara Falls on the US border with Canada and were overwhelmed by the sheer beauty and power of this magnificent part of God's creation.

On their return to Stanley, Kathleen began working on a project that had been in her mind for some years. She set about planning a Preparatory School for primary or elementary aged boys. As the College magazine later recounted:

> Mrs Martin cheerfully undertook the brunt of it. She thought out the plan of the building with the Architect, Mr I. N. Chau. She obtained a splendid staff with the help of devoted friends and . . . helped to draw up the system and regulations. Perhaps the zenith of her powers was reached here . . . Her interest in each individual child at the Preparatory School was characteristic . . . devoting hours to teaching backward boys to read English. She taught every single boy in the Prep. School, who could not do so, to swim. Her care of the children, while swimming, was lynx-eyed: she watched each one, all the time. She also started the Cubs, and under Mr Job's leadership gave her whole heart and energy to them.[39]

This new venture was a God-given opportunity to reach more families and so expand the influence of the College. As she thought about it, Kathleen realized that during her thirty years in Hong Kong she had now contributed to the development of five growing schools.

---

37. In November 1934, Bishop Lander died suddenly in London at the age of 73. Dorothy and Evan were grateful that Kitty and Arthur were able to represent them at the funeral.

38. *The Chimes*, 36. 2, 1947, 11.

39. *The Chimes*, 36. 2, 1947, 10–11.

On the morning of 7 July 1937, Japanese forces crossed the border from Manchuria and began a full-scale offensive that soon threatened Shanghai in the adjoining province. Six weeks later, the battle for the so-called 'Paris of the East' started with constant air raids and heavy naval bombardment. This onslaught was followed by infantry attacks that led to violent street-to-street fighting over the next two months. Though, for the time being, the Japanese recognized the neutrality of the International Settlement, Hong Kong newspapers reported the conflict in great detail, bringing war closer to the Colony's doorstep.

In the second half of 1937 calamity struck Hong Kong from another direction.

> "Wave after wave of disaster hit the city in late summer and autumn. First came an unnamed typhoon, gusting in on 1 September, with winds so strong that the Hong Kong observatory was incapable of registering its true strength, its instruments unable to visit wind velocity beyond 200 km/h. Boats upended, buildings and entire streets were destroyed, whole villages swept away by tidal waves [and 11,000 fatalities]. Then came fire, sweeping through slums and grand shoreline districts alike, taking lives, destroying homes, shops and hotels, and leaving hospitals overwhelmed. There followed epidemics, first cholera, then typhoid and malaria." [40]

While all this was happening, hundreds of thousands of refugees from the Mainland began pouring into Hong Kong. Most of these were escaping the escalating war in China. The Happy Valley racecourse became a huge tent camp, fed by handouts from the Government and Red Cross, as did certain other venues around the city including Hankow Barracks and the Central British School. Among the few institutions affected by both the war in China and the influx of refugees were schools. At St Stephen's, Ernest records that "In 1937 when hostilities began out here, and half our boys left us, we were providentially saved by the refugees who more than filled the school." [41] Though, less dramatically, St Paul's had a similar experience. The downside of the influx of these refugee students was dealing with the mental and emotional scars that they brought with them. Many had witnessed horrors that no child should ever live through. Their response to these experiences would be classified today as Post Traumatic Stress Disorder.

---

40. *South China Morning Post Magazine*, 9 August 2020. At https://www.scmp.com

41. E. Martin, Letter, 28 October 1939, 2 in *East Asia General: Japan and China: War Measures*, 1939–1945.

Living Through Troubled Times (1925–1938) 117

To escape the pressures of the College, Evan, Dorothy and Michael liked to get away as often as possible. They especially enjoyed traveling in their small Austin car to Repulse Bay, the island's most attractive beach on the south coast. There they rented a large bamboo mat-shed, with a covered verandah, two changing rooms, and a tiny kitchen. Evan sometimes took Michael for long walks in the hills of the New Territories. Commenting on his childhood, Michael recalls how Evan also "taught me to swim and surf, and took me to the College's gymnasium in the evenings. I enjoyed it all. He was not very impressed with the teaching I was receiving at the 'Peak School', so also taught me at home and on our walks. He did it in such an interesting way that I did not see it as 'teaching' and so enjoyed it."[42]

Early in 1938, much to Kathleen's delight, the Preparatory School finally opened its first building, which comprised a boarding house, dining hall, and classrooms. For the present, there was only room for nine boys. Alongside supervising the new school, Kathleen "continued to teach Geography and her students obtained distinctions in the Hong Kong University Examination . . . she took an enthusiastic interest in school sports, spending many an afternoon watching football matches or athletic contests. She taught many students their first tennis, including W. C. Choy . . . a [future] Davis Cup player."[43] Kathleen also learned to drive a car, often transporting students and staff to and from the city.

Ernest encouraged his staff at St Stephen's to be involved in more than the students' academic and sporting activities. Teachers not only helped organize regular concerts but also performed in them. In one such event, Ernest played a Showman, Kathleen a Flower Girl, and another teacher, Jack Asche, Snow White! Money raised would go to worthy causes like the School for the Deaf and Dumb in Kowloon.[44]

Towards the end of 1938, Kathleen and Ernest prepared for an eight-month long leave to mark his 10th anniversary as Headmaster, which included visits to Old Boys in China, the US, and the UK. During their time away, two Australian CMS missionaries were able to take over their responsibilities. Jack Asche became Acting Headmaster, and Nora Dillon, who had recently fled from Canton during Japanese air raids, took over Kathleen's role at the Prep. School.[45] In February 1939, the Martins traveled by the *President Taft*, and then *City of Los Angeles*, to San Francisco and Los

42. From personal correspondence with Michael Stewart.
43. *The Chimes*, 36. 2, 1947, 10.
44. See under 'Concerts' in *The Chimes*, 33. 1, 1939 and 33. 2, 1939.
45. For a full account of Nora Dillon's service in China, see Banks and Banks, *Through the Valley of the Shadow*, 92–115.

Angeles respectively. This not only gave them opportunity to see something of the West Coast of the US for the first time but to visit a few ex-students. After three weeks, they sailed via the Panama Canal to New York, from where they visited Old Boys studying at universities in Michigan and Massachusetts. Crossing the Atlantic to stay with family in London, they were able to connect with a dozen alumni studying and working in the UK. While they were there, Hitler's advances into Czechoslovakia and the Sudetenland, and potential move against Poland, increased anxieties about the possibility of war with Germany. In August the Martins began their return trip, stopping in Shanghai. Staying in the International Settlement, they were able to safely meet up with a few alumni, but found it impossible to locate others who had become refugees or joined the army.[46]

Ernest and Kathleen in the late 1930s

46. By now, four ex-students of the College had attained the rank of General in the Chinese forces, with several others in significant combat or support positions.

6

War Erupts on the Home Front
(1939–1945)

IN LATE FEBRUARY 1939, people in Hong Kong were made more aware of the armed conflict on their doorstep. The New Territories experienced a surprise air raid—in which two Chinese died and a few bombs hit a British area—for which the Japanese later apologized. On 4 May, the Hong Kong Government issued an advance paper, 'The Evacuation Scheme for the Colony of Hong Kong', focussing on "all women and children other than those of Chinese and enemy races, and those specifically registered for war or with no children living in the Colony."[1] Later that month, a P&O Liner in the vicinity was stopped and boarded by personnel from a Japanese destroyer, until the HMS *Duchess* arrived and ordered them to leave. In June, news broke that Swatow, only one hundred and seventy-five miles away, was now occupied by Japanese forces. By summer, training of nurses and air raid wardens gathered pace, and residents were encouraged to practice blackouts. In mid-August, seventeen Japanese bombers flew over the village of Stanley and, a week later, the First Battery of the Hong Kong Volunteer Defence Force was called up. An Emergency Powers Bill was also passed by the Government. While, according to the local press, Hong Kong was not in danger of an attack, public opinion was gradually forming the view that the war eventually would come their way.[2]

---

1. Banham, *Evacuation of Women and Children*, 16.
2. This is drawn largely from a diary kept by Barbara Anslow in Hong Kong at the time. See Gwulo: Old Hong Kong. At https://www.gwolo.com>node.

That summer, Evan, Dorothy, and Michael went on local leave to Dalat, a hill station in the south of Vietnam, at the time under French control. On 3 September, Britain declared war on Germany. Evan, being an officer in the HKVDC, was immediately called back to Hong Kong. As other ships were being commandeered for the military, Dorothy and Michael had to wait until a boat became free for civilian use. On this same historic day, Kathleen and Ernest arrived back in Hong Kong.

The outbreak of the war in Europe did not initially have any major impact upon Hong Kong, and while the Japanese had won some victories in China, their advance was presently halted. Appointing a Director of Evacuations was delayed for six months and, apart from some overseas diplomatic forays, no local preparations were made well into the following year.[3] Throughout that period, the main difference in life at St Paul's and St Stephen's was the exodus of some students to their families on the Mainland and influx of others whose parents sought refuge in Hong Kong. Evan and Dorothy did talk about the possibility that, if the Japanese invaded, they could be separated for quite a while. Knowing this, they made the most of their time together as a family. Despite Ernest's concern for her safety, Kathleen felt that anyone with experience as a nurse would be needed if trouble eventually came to Hong Kong.

In June 1940, the Japanese Navy began to harass fishing vessels, and also occupied two small islands off the coast of Hong Kong. The following month, after confirmation that Australia would take in evacuees, the first contingent of over sixteen hundred British Regular Army and Navy wives and children formed. Dorothy and Michael received word that on 5 July they would be leaving on the (somewhat ironically) *Empress of Japan* for Manila. Assembling at the Hong Kong Club, passports were checked and stamped 'Hong Kong Official Evacuee 1940', and from there they were taken by bus to the Star Ferry. After arriving in Kowloon, they boarded a further bus to No. 5 Wharf. Police officers assisted their boarding the ship, where passengers were crowded either into cabins or dormitory-style accommodation in the lower decks. After leaving Victoria Harbour, the ship encountered a storm and took two days to reach Manila, disembarking the next morning. As Michael Stewart writes:

> My mother and I were only allowed to take with us on the ship one suitcase each, so had to leave behind nearly all our clothes, family photograph albums, pictures, books, toys, furniture, silver, jewellery, etc . . . we stayed with my Uncle John Lander

---

3. On the war and post-war years in the Colony see Carroll, *Short History of Hong Kong*, 116–139.

...We were expecting to be able to return to Hong Kong soon but after a month or two we were again evacuated, to Australia ... our overcrowded ship [a Dutch liner *Johann De Witt*] arrived in Sydney and we were driven by members of the Women's Royal Voluntary Service to hotels where we were billeted... The hotel we were sent to at the southern edge of Bondi Beach ... was fine but living in one room was not, so we moved out as soon as we were allowed to and took a house near Rose Bay, sharing with Hong Kong friends ... I was then sent to Cranbrook School...[4]

Their arrival in Australia coincided with the beginning of the systematic and prolonged bombing of London, known as the Blitz, by the German Luftwaffe. This took place after the evacuation of retreating British forces from Dunkirk, and was a prelude to the intended invasion of England by the German Army. Arthur, whose church was only a few miles from central London, describes the impact of the nightly air raids over the next eight months, in which twenty-four high explosive bombs fell on Canonbury.

New Barnet had its share of bombs and incendiaries and twice we had our windows broken... With the evacuation of children [to the country] and the call-up of young people, the promising work among the youth fizzled out almost, and the nightly black-out and frequent air raid alarms made church services a matter of difficulty and strain, and house to house visiting became almost impossible since so many were busy and were not at home—except the sick and the elderly. The loss of our Church Hall, taken over as a First Aid Post, was a serious one, crippling our Sunday School work and making it difficult to carry on the social side. Perhaps the most cheering memory I have of those years is of the Prayer Groups which we started after the first National Day of Prayer in May 1940 [with] as many as ten groups meeting each week."[5]

大屠殺中倖存的孩子們

Around this time, their son Jim joined the Royal Air Force Bomber Command, in which life expectancy was generally short.

---

4. Banham, *Evacuation*, 32–33. This ship was the seventh of eight bringing women and children from Hong Kong to Australia.

5. A. Stewart, After Seventy Years, 17.

A few miles away, Reg and Mildred at St Bartholomew's in Islington, experienced their share of air raid destruction. When other ministers were finding reasons to move out of this hard-hit area, the Taylors courageously decided to stay. At the height of the Blitz, from January to April 1941, Reg kept a diary detailing their everyday personal life and responsibilities during the bombing.[6] Their church in Shepperton Road was struck by a bomb, which partly destroyed the building and also shook the Vicarage. Over the next few months, many parts of Islington began to look like a battlefield. Reg continued to hold services in the damaged church, and the two of them did "sterling work with parishioners who had to shelter from the bombing and with those who had been bombed out of their homes."[7] Altogether in Islington and its adjoining borough, nearly eight hundred civilians were killed by enemy aircraft attacks during the eight months the Blitz lasted.

Air raid damage in Islington during Blitz

Their son Lionel, having graduated from his father's alma mater, Emmanuel College, Cambridge, moved back home and took up the position of house surgeon at a hospital in London. Their daughter Kathleen had also hoped to study medicine but, as on a clergyman's wage there were insufficient funds for both to train as doctors, she decided to take up physiotherapy instead. In mid-1941, Mildred and Reg were delighted to hear from C.

---

6. This is held in the London Metropolitan Archives. See LMA P83/BAT/015.
7. From personal correspondence with grandson, David Taylor.

T. Song in Chengtu that on his first visit as Bishop to their mission station, he and his wife had "thought often" of them and their children, and that "their life and work in Chongkiang were still remembered and treasured."[8] In November that year, Lionel joined the Royal Naval Volunteer Reserve as a temporary surgeon lieutenant. He served throughout the remaining years of the war in destroyers, mainly in the Mediterranean.

With London suffering under heavy bombing, Philip and Nina decided he should come out of retirement, and move from Northern Ireland to take up a position at Kingston-upon-Thames Hospital in southeast London. During the Great War much of this had been turned into a military hospital. Though the move placed them, and seven year old Mary Louisa, in direct danger from air raids, they believed his wartime experience would be invaluable in dealing with civilian casualties. Throughout the eight months long Blitz, nearly five hundred bombs were dropped by the Luftwaffe on local factories, communication links, and public utilities in Kingston, including the Outpatients Department at his Hospital. A number of people were injured or killed, and some houses flattened. With the Stewarts and Taylors living less than ten miles away in north London, Philip and Nina were pleased to be near family once more.

For many years, Evan had been helping the HKVDC to improve its efficiency and readiness for any potential conflict. As a distinguished member of it later said: "This was one of the great periods of the Hong Kong Volunteers. It was a period of great recruiting activity and much development within the Corps, and Evan was in the thick of it all, particularly when there was anything to be done."[9] With the Japanese intruding ever closer to the Colony, the Corps was now involved in preparations in case of invasion.

> We spent most of our time in that last year before the War digging machine gun emplacements and trenches on the hillsides above such places as Magazine Gap, Wanchai Gap and Middle Gap . . . We were a very happy crowd in No.3 Company.[10]

---

8. See *Bulletin of the Diocese*, January 1941, 5.

9. Stewart, Hong Kong *Hong Volunteers*, 2020, Appendix VIII, entry by Lindsay Ride.

10. Stewart, *Hong Kong Volunteers*, 2020, Appendix VIII, entry by Bevan Field.

Group of Volunteer Defence Force, 1940

Apart from the HKVDC efforts, the only change in the Colony's military capabilities was the arrival of two thousand Canadian troops in mid-November 1941. The overall military strength in Hong Kong, however, remained extremely weak. Its army was primarily focussed on artillery, its naval presence had been weakened, and its air force was only token. The Colony was so isolated from other outposts of the Empire, that its small garrison had to include every kind of military unit—police, signallers, and engineers, to doctors, dentists and pay corps. There were only four infantry battalions, the 2nd/14th Punjabis, the 5th/7th Rajputis, the 2nd Royal Scots, and 1st Middlesex, as well as the HKVDC.

Unfortunately, some Japanese in the Colony, with the willing or coerced help of local Chinese, had already identified the nature, strength, and position of Hong Kong's defensive forces. In parts of the Colony, such as Kowloon, a small number of fifth columnists and criminal triads were also prepared to take advantage of any conflict that occurred. The inherent limitations of the Allied forces were described by Evan in the preface to his detailed account of the HKVDC in the battle of Hong Kong:

> We were lamentably weak as regards air power; we had few anti-aircraft batteries, and those we had were very short of ammunition for training purposes; we had no radio-location equipment; the infantry battalions were, until just before the actual outbreak of war, without mortars, weapons on which the enemy largely relied... Our inability to make air reconnaissance was a serious handicap; our only knowledge of enemy dispositions and troop

movements was obtained from ground observation, and was limited to such enemy forces as were actually in contact with our troops. The impossibility of making sea reconnaissance, and our consequent uncertainty about the safety of the south coast of the island necessitated our keeping troops in places where enemy landings might be made. This reduced the number of troops available as reserves for counterattack... In addition to the advantages the enemy had in complete sea and air domination, and their enormous preponderance in artillery, they had considerable superiority in the number of fighting men. They put into the field three divisions against our two brigades... The enemy had complete maps of the island, on which our fixed positions were shown. On both mainland and island Japanese troops were led by local guides, sometimes willingly, often under compulsion.[11]

大屠殺中倖存的孩子們

The Battle of Hong Kong commenced as news came of the Japanese air attack on Pearl Harbor—8 December local time. Soldiers crossed into the New Territories in several places, and twelve aircraft bombed Kai Tak airfield in Kowloon, destroying the only five RAF planes in the Colony. British intelligence believed there were only five thousand enemy troops across the border, whereas there were at least eight times that number of battle-hardened professional soldiers from the war in China. The first line of defense was the so-called Gin Drinkers Line that crossed the peninsula just below the hills bordering China. It was estimated that the defenders could hold off an enemy assault for a week. However, its centrepiece the Shing Mun Redoubt, a group of pill-boxes linked by underground tunnels, was overrun early morning on 10 December. The major part of the Japanese army then marched along the main road to the town of Tai-po, just over twelve miles north of Kowloon, while a smaller force crossed the river on the other side of the peninsula and also headed south. As the speed of the assault was so unexpected, all those who could use a rifle were handed one, while others scrambled for a place on ferries and boats across Victoria Harbour to Hong Kong Island. Occupying Kowloon the next day, the Japanese paraded captured British troops through its streets and declared all Chinese women

---

11. Stewart, *Hong Kong Volunteers*, 2005, 3–4. See further Banham, *Not the Slightest Chance*, whose title echoes a statement by Winston Churchill about the defense of Hong Kong.

prostitutes. Screams from victims of the resulting pillage and rape sounded across the Harbour to the Island all night long.

Half-way up the Kowloon peninsula, just off the shoreline, Evan was in charge of two platoons of the 3rd Machine Gun Company on Stonecutter's Island. Its task was to provide beach defense, as well as cross-fire protection for artillery units facing the enemy in the New Territories. Evan wrote how "The island had suffered continual shelling and bombing for three days, and practically every building had been hit, but the casualties were surprisingly small. No. 3 Company had lost only four wounded."[12] A member of his Company recorded that:

> One day on Stonecutter's, most of us had never been under fire before and, I must confess it does take some getting used to . . . the shells would come over three at a time, like steam engines, and crash into the island. Once when the shelling in the West Battery area was particularly bad I was on my way back to Company Headquarters near South Pier. As I got nearer to where the shells were coming down I kept one eye on the next handy bit of cover all the time, ready to dive for it at a moment's notice, and feeling very far from happy. Then I heard voices coming along the path, and there was Evan with a couple of Volunteers, strolling along as if the War was a thousand miles away. I was glad to see him and much comforted. We stood and chatted for a few moments and in that time three more shells came over. I'm afraid I crouched down instinctively, but Evan just stood there as if he was visiting . . . on a training afternoon before the balloon went up. When I straightened up again, feeling rather ashamed of myself, he just went on talking as if nothing had happened. I had a warm feeling of deep gratitude and respect, respect for his coolness and gratitude for not noticing. After that I felt better about the shelling and soon realised with a kind of happy relief that I was not going to be so scared after all. Evan had somehow in his kindly magic way given me sufficient of his own courage and trust to carry me through the days to follow.[13]

On 11 December, the troops on Stonecutter's Island were ordered to withdraw. Under heavy Japanese shelling, and without any Allied air or naval support, Evan played a major part in organizing their retreat. Without regard to his safety, he led their escape on a motor torpedo boat the twelve

---

12. Stewart, *Hong Kong Volunteers*, 2005, 13. On this action see also Matthews & Cheung. *Dispersal and Renewal*, 231.

13. See Stewart, *Hong Kong Volunteers*, 2020, Appendix VIII, entry by Bevan Field.

miles to Hong Kong Island.[14] The next day there was a mass evacuation of troops and civilians from Kowloon to the Island. To defend it from invasion, British forces were then divided into two Brigades, east and west of Causeway Bay. Evan's Company was transferred to Jardine's Lookout, above Wanchai (or Wang Nei Chong) Gap guarding the route to Stanley, where it had earlier dug trenches and built gun emplacements. For the best part of the next week, British positions were subjected to intense shelling and bombing as the Japanese prepared to invade the Island. Leaflets were dropped on British forces, and formal requests made to the British Command, urging surrender, but these were met with a resounding denial.

The invasion began on 18 December. The Japanese crossed the Harbour at three different points and soon gained ground in the area towards Wanchai Gap. As one of his men recalled:

> News of the landing was received at 10.30pm by our company commander, Major Evan Stewart, who found it difficult to convince Brigade HQ that the enemy were already in the vicinity. Soon there was no doubting their presence for in the dark we could hear shouting in Japanese. Closer contact led to several hours of fierce combat throughout the rainy night and misty dawn. . . . Early in the morning . . . the rest of the Company [was] deeply engaged on all fronts . . .[15]
>
> [According to another soldier] Evan was in the Headquarters battle shelter just west and below the Anti-Aircraft emplacement. He took a rifle and went up the stepped path to see what was going on. The A.A. people in the emplacement there were taking heavy punishments from small arms and mortar fire, and within a few moments Evan had been shot through the right shoulder. He promptly brought up his rifle and returned the fire, but the shock of the recoil on his damaged shoulder was enough for even such a man and they got him back to the battle shelter where they patched him up a little.[16]

By the end of the day, the Japanese were in control and the British had suffered nearly five hundred casualties, the majority in the Wong Nei Chong area. No.3 Company had suffered five casualties including forty-four deaths. Two of its four officers had been killed, the other two wounded. For three days, Evan managed to hide in a shelter with six others.

14. Kua, *Scouting in Hong Kong*, 229.
15. Matthews and Cheung, *Dispersal and Renewal*, 232.
16. Stewart, *Hong Kong Volunteers*, 2020, Appendix VIII, entry by Bevan Field.

Enemy soldiers were all round but did not go down to the shelter, possibly because it was on the exposed side of the hill. They never thought of coming out and surrendering. What they hoped for was a counterattack and they were ready to join in. But [as they were running out of food and ammunition] at last they had to accept the fact that the counterattack was not coming, and on the third night they left in pairs, at fifteen-minute intervals, quietly slid over the wall in front of the shelters and down the steep hillside to Happy Valley. Evan, typically, was the last to leave, and he was lucky to get away because by that time the sentries were suspicious and opened fire at the slight noise he made getting over the wall. Fortunately, it was a pitch-black night and he was not hit.

Evan got his shoulder cleaned up at the Hong Kong Hotel dressing station, and then with his arm in a sling went straight off to find the remnants of No. 3 Company, hardly a Platoon strong, holding part of the line in Wong Nei Chong. By that time, he had been almost constantly awake, and for much of the time under fire or in close contact with the enemy, for thirteen days. Wounded and in considerable discomfort, yet he was still not satisfied with a purely defensive role . . . phoned Volunteer Headquarters . . . asking to be put back into the battle!"[17] Along with a few other members of his Company, he was promptly assigned to another unit.

In Stanley, Kathleen and Ernest knew there were Army units deployed to protect the area from possible invasion by sea. They had already made contact with Kitty and Dorothy's step-brother, John Lander, who was stationed in one of the gunnery sections in Fort Stanley. On Monday 8 December, the first day of 'the battle for Hong Kong', Ernest:

> . . was holding a Staff Meeting to arrange the re-opening of the School the next day. About 75 boarders were there with them for the holidays: 16 older ones joined up at once for Ambulance service. A meeting of clergy and minsters was held, and arrangements made, with the Governor's consent, for English and Chinese padres to be visiting-Chaplains in the hospitals nearest them. Lists were made of hospitals and First-Aid Stations. Mrs. Martin was made supervisor of the Tweed Bay Hospital, Stanley, which formerly had been accommodation for prison warders. All the drugs and equipment had to be collected from

---

17. Stewart, *Hong Kong Volunteers*, 2020, Appendix VIII, entry by Bevan Field.

the principal M.O., and cooks and servants enlisted from the College servants. [18]

For the next few days, the Martins were able to drive into central Hong Kong, even though shells and bombs regularly fell around the city. The war came closer when they heard about the death of a staff member, Arthur Job, who was killed while defending Kowloon on 12 December. Over the next week, daily newspaper reports kept them in touch with what was happening and, after the fall of Kowloon, they were able to follow the course of the battle through radio bulletins of local and, sometimes, BBC news. From later broadcasts, they concluded that Evan's Company would have been overrun in the fighting, but had no idea of what had happened to him. Bodies struck by bombs began arriving in vans from the city, the first of which Ernest and Kathleen had to carry and bury, digging the graves themselves until others could be organized to help. A few days before Christmas, when Tweed Bay Hospital suffered air raid damage, the space adjoining the College's school hall was turned into a temporary field hospital. Its floor was covered with beds for wounded British, Canadian, and Indian soldiers, whose numbers grew as the fighting reached nearby Repulse Bay and then the Stanley Peninsula. One night, when the Martins were listening to the news on their radio with some local Chinese, bombs began to drop perilously near, one exploding about fifty yards from their quarters. As deaths mounted and shelling increased, each night "Mr and Mrs Martin, this time with the help of their gardeners, dug the first graves, reopening the old Military Cemetery of 1841."[19] By now most of the teachers had sought refuge elsewhere on the Island, leaving only a Chinese teacher Tam Chueng Huen, a few amahs, and assistants.

On Christmas Eve, the remaining fifty boarders at SSC were sent to bed at 6.30pm, and as the fighting escalated that night Ernest and Kathleen patrolled the hostel building, which lay between the opposing forces. After being raked by machine guns and blasted by hand grenades, around 4.30am it was attacked by nearly two hundred enemy soldiers and captured.

> The Japanese arrested the Martins and placed them in a two-boys bedroom, with their hands tied behind their backs, and a loop from them round their necks. Their wrists were tied to the end of the iron bed. They managed to squat on their suitcases side by side. Every few minutes, for the next twelve hours, some soldier molested them, slapping, punching, kicking, burning with a cigarette, pricking with bayonet or sword. (The Japanese

18. South China Mission, *CMS Historical Record*, 1945–1946, 350.
19. South China Mission, *CMS Historical Record*, 1945–1946, 350.

left them for a while and Kathleen feared that thy would cut her fingers off in order to steal her rings. Ernest, by a superhuman effort, managed to wriggle close enough to remove them). One soldier began to tear her dress, but Ernest gave a yell which made him desist, only to return with an evil-looking friend. They started the same thing again, and he yelled again, which infuriated them. One swung his rifle with both hands and full force striking Kathleen's leg above the knee with the butt of the rifle. Then they rammed with the butt of their rifles five or six times, striking them over the left ear and more or less knocking them out. Both of them fell forward to strangle on the loop around their necks, and the soldiers withdrew thinking they were finished. But they managed to struggle back to their seats. At 4.30pm they were moved into a small room (13 x 10 feet) with four British soldiers and ten Indians, all tightly trussed with ropes. The next afternoon, about the same hour, they were allowed to go to Tweed Bay Hospital, after being tied up without food or drink for thirty-six hours. Kathleen had very sore wrists and a terrible black eye.[20]

Ernest was convinced that they owed their lives to the Japanese thinking they had been beaten to death.

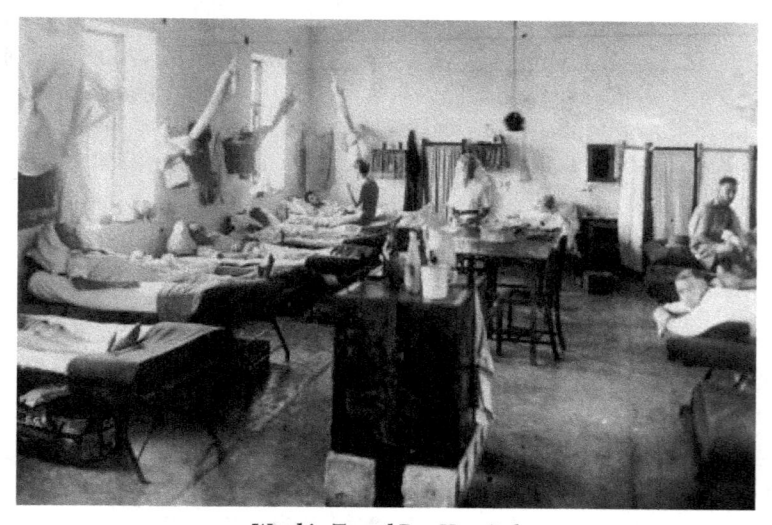

Ward in Tweed Bay Hospital

20. This report, which only personalizes their names, comes from E. Martin, Annual Letter, September 1945, 1–3, which was largely reproduced in the 'South China Mission', *CMS Historical Record*, 1945–1946, 351–332, with one additional detail (in brackets) from in the British Army Aid Group Reports and Weekly Intelligence Summaries, *Gwulo Old Hong Kong*, 21 August 1942.

War Erupts on the Home Front (1939–1945)

As soon as Kathleen and Ernest reached the hospital, they heard that Governor Mark Young had surrendered to the Japanese at 3.15pm the previous afternoon, Christmas Day. They also heard about a horrendous atrocity that had occurred among the patients and nurses inside the St Stephen's makeshift wards during the hours they were being interrogated.

> "On Christmas morning, while the fighting was still continuing along the ridge, about a hundred and fifty or two hundred Japanese broke into the hospital. They started bayoneting the wounded men, driving their bayonets repeatedly through bodies and mattresses. Lieut.-Colonel Black and Captain Whitney [both doctors] went forward in an endeavour to stop them. Black tried to bar the doorway to prevent more Japanese entering. He was shot through the head and bayoneted dozens of times as he lay on the ground. Whitney was also shot and then bayoneted repeatedly. The massacre continued until 56 of the patients in the hall had been stabbed to death. The others concealed themselves under beds and in dark corners.
>
> In the morning the surviving wounded were driven upstairs at the point of a bayonet and, together with the hospital orderlies, confined in one small room. There were in all about forty of them. Throughout the day, at intervals, men were taken out, one by one and butchered. Two or three of the seriously wounded men died in the room. At 1700 hours, a Japanese officer came in and told them they were very lucky—"Hong Kong has surrendered; if not, all will be killed." After dark all the wounded men who could stand were forced at the point of the bayonet to carry out the bodies of their murdered comrades and the blood-soaked mattresses to a great fire, which had been made from broken school desks.
>
> Still more horrible was the treatment of the women, all of whom were wearing Nurses' uniform and Red Cross armbands. They were confined in a small room upstairs. The four Chinese nurses were raped by Japanese soldiers repeatedly, then taken away, and have not been seen since. Three of the British nurses were also taken away at intervals and their dead bodies were seen next day. The other four were raped again and again throughout the morning and afternoon. In the evening a Japanese officer told them that they were lucky Hong Kong had surrendered; for in another hour they would have been dead. The four nurses did what they could for the few wounded men who had survived the massacre.[21]

21. E. Stewart, *Hong Kong Volunteers*, 53–54. An excellent Canadian documentary,

Together with medical staff, and other soldiers killed in defense of Stanley, over one hundred bodies were burned by the Japanese.

Ernest and Kathleen were also shaken when they heard about the execution of their Chinese colleague, Tam Cheung Huen, who had been trying to protect students. News that John Lander had been killed in fighting near the gate of St Stephen's College also deeply affected them. Once he had sufficiently recovered, Ernest sought help to find where the Japanese had cremated the bodies of St Stephen's staff and patients killed on Christmas Day. When these were located, "a casket was made, and one evening the Rev E. E. Martin held a short memorial service and buried them in the garden cemetery where many mounds and stones mark the graves of the early colonialists."[22] Over the following month, he went out daily and found the sites of about a hundred others killed in the fighting, and erected wooden crosses with names on them.

大屠殺中倖存的孩子們

After the surrender, enemy troops were largely allowed to run riot in central Hong Kong and Kowloon. There were many atrocities, including the rape of more than ten thousand Chinese women and teenagers.[23] Many, including students from both St Paul's and St Stephen's cluster of colleges, escaped to Free China and began serving in the army, hospitals, relief work, and the Red Cross.[24] In January 1942, the Japanese command decided to turn St Stephen's and the area around Stanley Gaol into Hong Kong's civilian internee camp. After securely fencing the boundary with barbed wire, and setting up an observation post on a small hill above it, all non-combatant 'enemy nationals' were ferried south to the Camp. Towards the end of January, two and a half thousand men, women and children, joined the Martins and a few other non-Chinese from the Village. Most of these were British subjects—including Canadians, Australians, New Zealanders, and a small number of Eurasians—along with around three hundred Indians, Dutch and Americans.[25] One of the internees was Leslie Puckle, a fifty-year-old nurse, whose husband had been in charge of Air Raid Prevention in the

---

containing an interview with a surviving soldier, is *A Savage Christmas: The Battle for Hong Kong*, dir. Brian McKenna, Gala Films, 1991.

22. 'South China Mission', *CMS Historical Record*, 1945–1946, 355.
23. See further Snow, *Fall of Hong Kong*, 77–90.
24. So, for example, Barker, *Change and Continuity*, 123.
25. Archdale and Kent, *Women's History Review*, 388.

Colony. Her detailed memoirs of time in Stanley Camp provide the best personal account of day to day life over the next three and a half years.²⁶

> Many of the buildings in the camp were badly damaged by shellfire. Also, the whole place had been thoroughly looted, first by the Japanese and then by the Chinese from Stanley village, so that it was a scene of devastation when we arrived . . . We were very lucky compared with some other camps, as our surroundings were most beautiful and we had quite a reasonable amount of space to walk about in outside, but once inside our quarters it was a different story. We were terribly overcrowded and the lack of privacy was for many of us the worst trial of camp life.

Inside dormitory at Stanley Internment Camp

> Life in those first weeks was rather a grim affair. Many women in camp had lost either husband or son in the fighting and others were still uncertain as to the fate of their relatives; practically everyone had lost all their worldly possessions and knew their homes to be looted and wrecked . . . Most of us were suffering subconsciously from shock and from a sense of unreality.

26. Puckle, 'Stanley Internment Camp', Gwulo. The following series of quotes come from her memoirs. The most exhaustive account of the Camp is provided by Banham, *Hong Kong Internment*, and there is also a set of eight audio interviews with its head Chaplain, Joseph Sandbach in the archives of the *Imperial War Museum*.

The Martins were allocated a room designed for two people which they had to share with four other internees. Each morning Kathleen would rise at six o'clock to cook rice-scones for everyone in their group, using only a small clay pot or 'chatty' over a dried grass fire.[27]

Since the number of internees far exceeded the facilities, initially everything was rather chaotic. Many didn't know what to do or where to go for the most basic necessities, and often had to wait in long queues for washing and toilet facilities, food and water, fuel, and power. A Temporary Council, consisting of business people, professionals and ministers, was established to do some basic planning. Ernest's knowledge of the layout and equipment of the College buildings was invaluable here. Sub-committees were then set up to manage the canteen, electricity, billeting, supplies, welfare, health, education, recreation, and religion. It took some time for life in the Camp to become organized.

> The food in those first weeks was simply unspeakable—all we were given was sodden, badly cooked rice, with a small heap of fish-bones and skin dumped on top, and a few coarse rank green vegetables. This was served to us twice a day, at eleven and five. In addition to this, we had a tiny slice of bread, often mouldy.
>
> The weather was cold and wretched and we had no heating of any sort. Many of us had not enough winter clothes and blankets to keep us warm; and this miserable diet began to tell its tale in pinched faces and hollow eyes, and . . . diseases such as [malaria], beri-beri, pellagra and worst of all central blindness, all of which were due to the lack of one or other of the vital vitamins in our diet . . . Dysentery also broke out at this time and for a while there was an epidemic of it . . . A hospital, and clinics in different parts of the camp were opened, and . . . wonderful work [was] done by both doctors and nurses in Stanley. Although, like all the internees, they were suffering from malnutrition and lack of vitality, with incredible difficulties to contend with owing to lack of medical supplies and drugs, they gave freely and unsparingly of their best.

Altogether the camp contained forty doctors, two dentists, six pharmacists, and a hundred fully qualified military nurses. There were also a large number of women from the Volunteer Nursing Detachment of the HKVDC, as well as from the Auxiliary Nurses Service.[28] As someone with both nursing and administrative experience, Kathleen was appointed as a

---

27. *The Chimes*, 36.2, 1947, 11.
28. Emerson, *Hong Kong Internment*, 98.

Supervisor at Tweed Bay Hospital, whose wards had seventy beds for the most serious cases. Ernest worked there also as a Hospital Chaplain.[29] They were also called in to deal with a wide range of domestic problems and broader disputes that regularly surfaced among internees. As Sarah Puckle notes:

> Camp life seemed to intensify whatever characteristics a man or woman possessed. Those who were unselfish and courageous became even more so, while others lost all self-respect and gave way to theft, scrounging, immorality and back-biting. In this connection I should like to say a word about the members of the various missionary societies, of whom we had many in Stanley. One often hears missionaries criticized, but I can only say that they were a shining example in our internment camp. Almost without exception they played their part in the communal life as doctors, nurses or teachers according to their capabilities. They were cheerful, helpful and uncomplaining, and undertook readily any unpleasant or distasteful task which had to be done. As a body they made a most noble contribution to the well-being of the community and their selfless work earned the admiration and respect of us all . . .
>
> The church was one of the first things to come into being, when in the very early days the ministers of the dozen or more denominations met and formed themselves into a body called the United Churches. Services were held every Sunday in SSCs's school hall, a choir was started, and the church became a very practical inspiration to the crowds who attended. Among the group of wider internees, there were at times some surprising turns to religion by individuals or couples.

As an Anglican minister, Ernest took his turn to lead services and preach, as well as occasionally conduct baptisms, funerals, and occasional weddings. An eyewitness described one typical sad occasion. "Rev Martin, shoes and rolled down socks showing under his oilskin, over his head a Chinese waxed paper umbrella, conducted the service . . . After the service was over, he hurried home. Only the police pall-bearers remained to remove the coffin which is used for every funeral."[30] Alongside services, there were also study, discussion, and prayer groups. Kathleen and Ernest took part in a weekly CMS prayer meeting with colleagues like Edna Atkins from St Stephen's Girls College, and Australians Rev Harry Wittenbach and his wife who had been teaching in Canton.

29. See, in part, 'South China Mission', *CMS Historical Record*, 1945–1946, 355.
30. Wright-Nooth, *Prisoner of the Turnip Heads*, 200–201.

By March 1942, rumors were circulating in Hong Kong that both Martins had been killed at St Stephen's. These reached CMS London through the Colonial Office, though a follow-up inquiry with Bishop Hall, now based in Szechwan, indicated that there were conflicting reports about their deaths. This ongoing uncertainty was painful, particularly for Arthur, Mildred, and Philip, especially as it took a further three years for the truth to be known and passed on to CMS readers.

Over the next year, conditions in the camp gradually improved. The weather became warmer, food supplies increased in response to protests, and kitchens were set up in different parts of the camp. Slowly a bewildered and unorganized crowd of people began to act as a community. As internees' particular abilities were recognized and utilized, the Camp became a self-supporting township with church, school, hospital, and social services. Every so often it benefited as parcels of clothing and supplies were sent into the Camp by the International Red Cross, and occasional food parcels and supportive messages were smuggled in from concerned people in Hong Kong at some risk.

> Schooling was begun, and under immense difficulties, owing to lack of space and proper equipment, the task of educating the children in camp was carried on. There was a Junior, Middle, and Senior School, staffed by teachers from . . . several educational institutions in the Colony. Libraries, too, were started in different parts of the camp, and no words can say what a boon they were . . . After a time a very fair library was assembled, and it provided endless interest and amusement for what would otherwise have been dreary and profitless hours. Lectures, too, were started on a wide variety of subjects, and we were lucky in having all the teaching staff of the Hong Kong University with us, so we had highly qualified and well-trained speakers to lecture us on subjects such as literature, biology, psychology and so on. Classes were also started in languages, both European and Asiatic. . .
>
> Nor was lighter entertainment neglected. We had a lot of extremely talented people in camp, and very soon concerts of both light and classical music were in full swing, and an Amateur Dramatic Society gave some really remarkable performances, overcoming successfully immense difficulties with regard to costumes and scenery. The plays ranged from Shakespeare to musical comedy and ballet, and not only provided many a pleasant hour's relief from tedium, but gave us a fresh topic of conversation, which was all too apt at that time to centre on food, or the lack of it, and the delinquencies of one's room-mates . . .

Kathleen and Ernest saw all these activities as important to harmonious life in the Camp, and were especially involved in those that drew on their skills as educators. Now and again they also took the opportunity to break down the stereotype of missionaries by taking part in revues, concerts and plays.

> [Mostly, the Japanese] did not obtrude themselves unduly into our daily life, and left the running of the camp to a certain extent to the internees themselves; though permission had to be obtained for every alteration in camp rules, and for the holding of every meeting or entertainment, which permission they often withheld, just to make themselves unpleasant and to let us know who was master . . . Face slapping and knocking down were of common occurrence; and people were frequently taken to the Japanese Administration headquarters and beaten up for some minor offence . . . Though not always in evidence, the Japanese were a sinister and menacing background to our lives, affecting every moment of our day, and obstructing every effort to improve our lot. Nothing that went on in camp was hidden from them, as their spies were everywhere, and our movements were watched through field-glasses from the Japanese Headquarters.

大屠殺中倖存的孩子們

After surrendering with his unit to the Japanese, Evan was one of around six thousand Allied soldiers held at Victoria Barracks on Hong Kong Island. The majority were destined for Sham Shui Po, a former refugee camp in Kowloon. Though still suffering from his shoulder wound, Evan was mobile enough to walk. On 29 December, the PoWs were gathered by their captors into units, taken across the harbor in ferries, and marched up to and then along Nathan Road to the Camp. Among this group was an Australian Lieutenant Colonel, Dr Lindsay Ride, Chief Medical Officer of the HKVDC, who knew Evan well, who wrote that:

"On arrival at Sham Shui Po we swarmed through the gates and were let loose just like a flock of sheep being driven into new fields . . . The state of the camp was almost indescribable . . . there were no windows or doors left in any of the huts. All furniture and beds, taps, basins, baths, cooking utensils etc. had been removed and most of the woodwork in the huts ruthlessly ripped off by looters."[31] For the next three months, Evan and his fellow

---

31. 'See 'Hong Kong Resistance'. At the time, Lindsay Ride was Professor of

prisoners had to sleep on bare concrete floors and put up sacking, tin and plaster board to keep the winter cold out. They also suffered from acute food shortages and medical supplies, as well as severe mistreatment by Japanese guards.

After a successful escape by four officers, including Lindsay Ride, across the border to Free China, the remaining six hundred officers in Sham Shui Po, and a hundred other ranks acting as cooks and orderlies, were moved to another camp. As one PoW remembered: "When we started on our walk through the streets of Kowloon that afternoon in April, we did not know where we were going, but after covering about three miles we arrived at Argyle Street Camp, near Kai Tek. There was no sign of life on the streets, and shop windows were shattered and everywhere appeared to be looted."[32] The compound itself contained simple rows of bare huts surrounded by triple barbed-wire, electric fences, and flood lamps to prevent escape.

The Argyle St Camp was in very poor repair. Food was inadequate and its nutritional value nil; there were no amenities, facilities, or medical equipment. Though there was a Japanese doctor:

> " . . . he did not provide any medical help at all. When Evan's untreated wounds became too painful, he would sometimes ask a friend to knock him out. His wounds may have been a blessing in disguise, as many PoWs deemed by the Japs to be fit were shipped off to be slave labourers in Japan. Many of them died from ill-treatment, malnutrition or over-work. Others drowned, or were shot escaping, when in October 1942 the *Lisbon Maru* was inadvertently sunk by an American submarine. [33]

In the camps, prisoners were viewed as contemptible for the very act of surrendering. Japanese guards were trained to regard the inhumane treatment of PoWs as deserved, since "real warriors" died in battle or committed suicide if likely to be captured. Officers, rather than being treated more respectfully because of their rank, were treated as even more contemptible than ordinary prisoners because they most of all should have acted 'honorably' in the samurai tradition. Since Evan received no treatment for his wounds, and lacked the proper nutrition necessary for healing, as time went on his condition worsened, resulting in constant pain.

However, Evan's move to Argyle St Camp had an unexpected benefit. Dorothy and Michael finally received word through the Red Cross that,

---

Physiology at Hong Kong University and Commander of the HKVDC.

32. Banham, *Hong Kong Internment*, 42.

33. From personal correspondence with Michael Stewart. The sinking of this ship, carrying around PoWs, is detailed in Banham, *Sinking of the Lisbon Maru*.

though wounded, he was alive. Although this was mixed news, hearing something official was a huge relief after six stressful months of waiting. Since the fall of Hong Kong, the salary they were receiving was not nearly enough to pay for their flat and Michael's school fees, so Dorothy had to find a job. (The UK Government offered loans to Hong Kong evacuees but, not knowing if Evan would survive the war, she did not want to be faced with big debts.) [34] Through friends, Dorothy found a position as a nursing sister at a large rural boarding school in Armidale, New South Wales. The Armidale School paid her a salary, provided accommodation, and included Michael's school fees.

Arthur and Kitty's son Jim enlisted in the Royal Air Force in 1941. After training in Canada, he was posted to a bomber squadron in Burma. By 1944 he was a Warrant Officer in the RAF at an airfield in Bangladesh. Four days after Christmas, he was the pilot on a mission to mine the Rangoon river estuary in Burma, which was then in Japanese hands. In bright moonlight, his low-flying plane was shot down by flak, and tragically all nine crew were killed. On New Year's Day, Arthur "seemed to hear a voice, 'Can you spare your Jim? Can you give him up?' I walked a while before I said 'Yes, Lord, I will', and after that there was not so much shock when the telegram arrived—'Regret to inform you.'" [35] News of the death of their son, who was only twenty-one, hit Kitty particularly hard, and for some months refused to believe he had been killed.

In Stanley Camp a year earlier, several internees were accused of passing intelligence to the British Army Aid Group [BAAG].[36.] As Puckle recorded:

> Japanese Secret Police swooped down on the camp, and arrested men and took them away—sometimes they returned after some weeks, forced under threats of re-arrest not to speak of their experiences to anyone; but very often they were not seen again. In October 1943, eight men were beheaded at Stanley, on a beach near the camp, in full view of a bungalow where the wife of one of the victims was living. These executions aroused the greatest horror and indignation in camp; but orders were given by the Japanese that no religious services were to be held for the

---

34. From personal correspondence with Michael Stewart.

35. A. Stewart, After Seventy Years, 17.

36. The BAAG was a resistance group set up by Dr Lindsay Ride after his escape to Free China. It became the chief source of military intelligence for the Allies in Southern China, helped liberate two thousand people from Japanese captivity, and smuggled medical supplies, food, and letters of encouragement into Hong Kong.

executed men and there were to be no public demonstrations of sympathy to their relatives, under threats of severe punishment.

[By the start of 1944] conditions became harder, the food more scarce and poorer in quality and the electricity was reduced steadily until finally it was cut off altogether. For the last year of our captivity we had no artificial light at all, and when the daylight failed we sat in the dark. This was not so bad in the summer, as we were allowed to sit outside until 9 o'clock, but in the winter it was dreary beyond words as we huddled on our beds in the dark, clad in our outdoor clothes for warmth and with no distraction but our thoughts . . . Worst of all, however, was the water shortage. The pumping at the reservoir was done by electricity and when the electric current failed owing to lack of fuel, we had continual trouble with the water supply. At one time the water mains were only turned on once in five days and as we had no containers in which to store water, the discomfort and inconvenience this entailed were beyond words. The attitude of the Japanese too became harsher and more domineering, rules and regulations were tightened up and penalties became more severe for any disregard of orders.

After nearly three years of stress, poor diet, and limited medications, one day while on garden duty, Kathleen felt severe chest pain and was taken to Tweed Bay Hospital. There she was diagnosed with an aneurism caused by arterio-sclerosis, a condition that blocks the blood flow to major organs. With Ernest by her side for much of the time, she remained in the ward for the next ten weeks, mostly on morphine to reduce the pain. Over this period, he often heard from visitors how much "her happy and Christlike character had made a deep impression on her fellow-internees,"[37] and was grateful that while in hospital, "her mind retained its strength and its faith, and she maintained her sweetness and her memorable smile."[38] On 19 January 1945, she finally died. It was reported by CMS that her funeral took place on 'a perfect Stanley day' in the quiet, century-old cemetery. Sharing the occasion with Ernest were many friends, colleagues, and well-wishers from the Camp. The day was marked by sadness mixed with subdued triumph.

"Few things have made a deeper impression on the average Stanley internee than her courage and cheerfulness in her long illness, and his attitude and bearing after her death."[39] At one point in the funeral "an unknown internee in St Stephen's College, with his cornet, sent the strains of 'Abide

---

37. Mentioned by Ernest to Mowll, *Memorable Nine Weeks*, 6.
38. *The Chimes*, 36.2, 1947, 12.
39. 'South China Mission', *CMS Historical Records*, 1945–1946, 353.

with me' ringing through the Great Hall and Rooms where Kathleen Martin had made her home for many years."⁴⁰

Kathleen's grave at Stanley Military Cemetery

A plaque was later erected at the College in Kathleen's honor. It read:

IN AFFECTIONATE MEMORY OF
KATHLEEN L. MARTIN
HONG KONG 1905–1945
ST STEPHEN'S COLLEGE 1921–1945
GIFTED WITH MANY A GRACE
AND GREATLY BELOVED

"THE PEOPLE THAT KNOW THEIR GOD
SHALL BE STRONG" DAN. XI.32.

40. *The Chimes*, 36.2, 1947, 12.

7

With an Eye to the Future (1945–1958)

DESPITE BEING ONLY FIFTEEN miles away on the other side of Hong Kong, Evan sadly knew nothing about Kathleen's death. Nine months earlier, all the officers in the Argyle St. Camp had been transferred back to a secure wired-off section in Sham Shui Po. Shortly after, a Japanese plane strafed the area " . . . and shot up the length of the wide road which ran through the camp. We all dived under our beds—an automatic though futile reaction—all except Evan, who apparently noticed nothing, but just sat on his bed and got on with some reading he was doing at the time. He was different from the rest of us."[1] Terribly thin from malnutrition, and in constant pain from his still untreated wounds, he was increasingly bed-ridden but, sustained by his faith, continued to encourage those around him.

V-J Day finally came on 15 August 1945, and four days later control of the Camp was handed over to the British. On surrender, a Japanese officer presented his sword to Evan as a mark of the highest respect for his actions in the defense of Hong Kong. Sham Shui Po began to receive visits by representatives from civic, welfare, medical, and religious organizations supplying food, clothing, and medicines. In early September, medical authorities assessed Evan as so severely ill that he needed specialist treatment overseas. He was assigned to a hospital ship bound for Australia, where he would be near Dorothy and Michael. Unfortunately, because there had been no mail in the camps, Evan did not know that six months earlier they had already

---

1. See Stewart, *Hong Kong Volunteers*, 2020, Appendix VIII, by Bevan Field, a fellow prisoner at the time.

left for England. Hearing this on arrival in Sydney, Evan remained with the ship as it was eventually bound for the UK.

At the beginning of August in Stanley Camp, hopes ran high that captivity would soon be at an end. "There was no outward excitement, no wild cheering or singing—only a dazed incredulous wondering whether it was really true that this moment for which we had longed for so many years had come at last."[2] Four days after V-J day, on Sunday 19 August, Ernest was involved in a Thanksgiving Service, attended by the whole camp. The crowd was so large that many had to group around the windows and doors outside the main hall. Next, planes dropped supplies and messages about how transfer from the Camp to people's homes would take place. During the whole time at Stanley, only one hundred and twenty people died. "When compared to the horrendous number of Allied servicemen who perished in the Japanese prisoner-of-war camps, and the brutality inflicted on the untold number of Chinese, the relatively small numbers of internees who died at Stanley is simply remarkable."[3] For the time being, Ernest decided to stay on in Stanley, but planned to visit England to see family.

When Evan's ship docked in Southampton, meeting up with Dorothy and Michael must have seemed like a miracle. An ambulance then took him to Stoke Mandeville Hospital in Aylesbury, fifty miles north-west from London. This state-of-the-art new hospital had been set up primarily for injured military personnel with spinal injuries. Over the next year, Evan received specialist therapy, which included surgery to remove fragments of shrapnel in his back, traction to stabilize and align the spine, and medication to reduce inflammation. Complementary therapies were applied to develop muscles and improve mobility, as well as use of sporting activities to build both mental and physical strength. Progress was slow yet steady, though leaving Evan permanently with a 'dropped foot'. This disability caused weakness, numbness, and pain in his foot muscles, and led to dragging the front of one foot when walking.

Buoyed by letters from Old Boys at St Paul's, and Dr Woo at the Girls College, as the year progressed Evan was increasingly looking forward to resuming his work in Hong Kong. After the Colony's liberation, Dr Woo had moved quickly to re-open not only the Girls but also the Boys College as one school. She did this partly to get education underway again as quickly as possible, partly because the SPC buildings had been trashed by the Japanese, and partly to prevent a Military Government take-over of their desirable properties in the heart of Hong Kong. A Provisional Joint Council was set

---

2. Puckle, 'Stanley Internment Camp', Gwulo.
3. Archdale and Kent, *Women in Stanley*, 388.

up, under the chairmanship of Bishop Hall, to oversee this co-educational enterprise for a trial period of three years.

On 7 October, Evan received word from the War Office that he had been awarded a Distinguished Service Order (DSO) for his gallantry during the Battle of Hong Kong. When he was well enough to return to the Colony, this honor was publicly conferred on him by the Governor of Hong Kong. The citation read:

> This officer commanded No. 3 Company, Hong Kong Volunteer Defence Corps, first on Stonecutters Island later in the Wong Nei Chong Gap area. The successful evacuation of Stonecutters while under fire was greatly due to his powers of organisation and leadership; while at Wong Nei Chong, although wounded early in the fighting, he continued to command his Company with a total disregard for his own safety and suffering. After the capture of Wong Nei Ching by the enemy he organised the escape of the six survivors from that area and finally found his own way back alone through the enemy lines. Throughout, his conduct was an example to all of high courage and coolness. During the fighting at Wong Nei Chong, Major Stewart's Company suffered 100% casualties in officers and over 80% in Other Ranks.

His 3rd Machine Gun Company's defensive action was considered so courageous and effective, that it was studied regularly by Army units stationed in Hong Kong for the next fifty years.

Arthur, now sixty-seven, was considering how much longer he and Kitty should stay in the parish, or perhaps move for a final tenure elsewhere. Only a few miles away, Reg and Mildred were already preparing to take up a new parish at All Saints, Longhope, in Gloucester. Then, as he wrote:

> "Like a bolt from the blue came a letter from the British Red Cross, inviting me to join a small party going to Hong Kong at the request of the Military Government to assist in the rehabilitation of the Chinese who were expected to pour back during the following months . . . On 1 November 1945 we took to the air . . . what a thrill it was to see Hong Kong again.
>
> My first impression was how little material damage there was. Compared with parts of London, bomb damage was slight. The worst damage was done by the Chinese themselves, and one cannot be surprised at this because the shortage of fuel was great, and so all empty buildings, schools, halls, etc. had been gutted of all woodwork. On the Peak not a house remained undamaged and in many cases roofs had collapsed and the buildings

were mere shells. Gardens, tennis-courts, hillsides, untended for nearly four years, were mere jungles ... Every church had been taken by the Japanese; the Cathedral had become a men's club; St Paul's was turned into a police training centre; St Andrew's became a Buddhist mausoleum; and Christ Church was handed over to the Japanese cavalry. In spite of all this church life had carried on ...

[My] social work was most cheering ... In various centres cooked rice was served free to several thousand people, mostly women and children, every afternoon, while a doctor examined everyone for disease. My job was to interview those who needed help. The biggest difficulty was to find things to give them. On one occasion we had several large sacks of old military clothing. ... After a few weeks in the Peninsula Hotel, accommodation was found for me in St Andrew's Vicarage, Kowloon ... I took one or two services every Sunday, but also took a share in weekly Bible Classes for Service Men ... I also preached occasionally in the Cathedral and in St Paul's Church.[4]

Arthur was also welcomed back to Hong Kong at a rally organized by the Old Boys of St Paul's. At this, several speakers complained that they had not been consulted about the decision to amalgamate the two schools, and felt that in the long term this was not in the best interests of the College. Arthur agreed that SPC should be re-opened as soon as practicable, but a further difficulty was that the Bishop wanted to put its land and buildings at Glenealy to other uses. On his return to England, Arthur promised to take up the matter with both Evan and CMS.

Back home in New Barnet, Arthur realized that he wanted to spend the final years of his ministry "in his beloved Hong Kong among his many friends there.[5] This was strengthened by his oldest daughter, Margaret's desire to teach in Hong Kong where she had spent her earliest years. Arthur wrote to St Stephen's "where Ernest Martin was transferring a concentration camp back into a school." To his surprise and delight, Ernest offered to find a position for both of them. Kitty felt she had to stay in England with Joan for a time before coming out herself. "My successor was appointed, those last weeks in Lyonsdown passed swiftly, and [we] boarded the P & O *Canton*. We had a good voyage. I could not help contrasting it with the first time and the thrill of it all just 42 years before." Since SSC was the first school Arthur had taught at, it felt like coming full circle, and enabled him to say

---

4. A. Stewart, After Seventy Years, 18–19.

5. This, and the following two short quotes, are also from A. Stewart, After Seventy Years, 19–20.

goodbye to Kathleen in the familiar surroundings of Stanley. Along with teaching high school students, he enjoyed providing adult education classes for College servants and their wives. Margaret joined the staff of St Stephen's Girls College as a kindergarten teacher, and felt it was a privilege to follow in Kathleen's footsteps there.[6]

Memorial Chapel Window to war victims at SSC

Unfortunately, Arthur had only been in Hong Kong a short time when he was diagnosed with dangerously high blood pressure. By that time Kitty had arrived, and fortunately his health soon improved. Not long after, the sad news reached them that Philip had died at home in Strangford, County Down. People at St Stephen's, and in Stanley Village, still remembered the care he had shown them during the malaria epidemic.[7]

大屠殺中倖存的孩子們

In April 1947, Evan and Dorothy finally returned to Hong Kong. Needing to replace all their possessions which had been looted during the war, it took a while for them to get back on their feet financially. For the first few

---

6. Barker, *Change and Continuity*, 128.

7. After her education in Ireland and England, Philip's daughter Mary Louisa married James Pooler. They also settled on a property in Strangford, where they bred horses, and raised a family involved in equestrian activities.

months, he was pleased to teach as just one of the staff at the Joint College and then, at the start of the next academic year, to become Deputy Principal during the three-year trial, after which the future of the two schools would be re-assessed.

> With the return of their beloved headmaster, the alumni had someone to rally around. However, the lack of suitable site and financing was among the difficulties preventing the re-opening of the College . . . In the Joint Council there were two persons, Dr Tso Seen Wann and Canon E. W. L. Martin who were very much in sympathy with the alumni and their aspiration to re-establish St Paul's College. Dr Tso was a member of the College Council since its last reconstruction in 1909 and a member of the Legislative Council. Canon Martin was married to Kathleen Stewart, the former headmistress of St Paul's Girls College . . . Their opinion carried much weight in the termination of the three year's trial period of the amalgamation of the two institutions. A formal protest bearing more than 300 signatures of the alumni was sent to England, demanding the re-opening of St Paul's College . . . and a fundraising Ball was organized by the Alumni Association . . . To pacify the alumni the Bishop offered the site of St John's Hall, a residential hall of the University of Hong Kong . . . to be the new site for St Paul's College, together with reasonable monetary compensation for the various buildings at Glenealy for the switch of sites.[8]

This arrangement allowed St Paul's to regain its identity, and for Evan, teachers, alumni, and students to start a new page in the history of the College. The Bishop jokingly suggested, as he had even before the war, that in view of Arthur and Evan's central role at St Paul's, it should be called 'Stewart College'![9]

The Old Boys soon raised additional money to purchase space that was empty in St John's because of its move to another site and, when its premises were fully vacated, to erect some new facilities. In September 1950, Evan proudly re-opened the doors of the reconstituted St Paul's College, with seven classes, two hundred and eighty boys, and all the pre-war teachers. Despite Dr Woo's decision to keep her institution co-educational, it did not take long for enrolments to reach their previous level. Again, Evan's approach was to mix with students in the playground and at sporting events. This led to their favorite Chinese name for him, 'bud tsai'. Most likely this refers to the fact that Evan "limped from being shot during the war: 'limped'

8. Fung, *From Devotion to Plurality*, 75–76.
9. Hall, "Confirmation and Ordination".

sounds like 跛 (bai) in Cantonese, which has similar pronunciation with 畢 (bud), while 仔 (tsai) means a young guy or son."[10]

In late 1950, Arthur suffered a slight stroke. He was writing the final part of his memoirs at the time, and stopped in mid-sentence, never to complete the manuscript. In the weeks that followed he suffered several more minor strokes, and the doctor ordered a return to England. Margaret wrote: "This was a great disappointment to him, because he had hoped to end his days in Hong Kong, among his many friends there."[11] In January 1951, he and Kitty boarded a ship for England and moved to Bournemouth, where for a while he was able to assist in the parish church. A year later, he suffered a major stroke, which confined him permanently to bed.

Over these years Evan and his staff found that educating this new generation of boys had distinct challenges. Many of them had received no formal schooling during the Occupation, so lacked basic knowledge and skills for their age. Another issue was lack of discipline due to the chaotic nature of life during that time. Still others, especially refugees from China, had served in the military and experienced some form of what is now called post-traumatic stress disorder.

Evan had re-joined the HKVDC after his return. Since it was now a decade since the Battle of Hong Kong, he felt it was time to write an account of the actions of the Corps. This was published in 1953, and soon became the recognized treatment of the whole conflict. As a teacher of History, he believed that preserving a record was essential to honoring the sacrifice of those who served, as well as avoiding mistakes of the past. The act of writing also probably helped him process some of the trauma experienced in the war. According to his colleagues in the Volunteers, however, Evan's "greatest work", was taking part in its post-war organization. "Military requirements had changed, the volunteer atmosphere was different, yet Evan's reply to the call was the same it had always been, despite his physical ability. The formation of the Hong Kong Regiment's Home Guard (HKRHG), development of their wonderful spirit and the success of their achievements, were all due to Evan and a few other stalwarts."[12]

Among the other positions he held was Chairman of both the Inter-School Sports Committee and of Hong Kong School Certificate Panel; Vice-Chairman of the Hong Kong Teachers Association; Member of the Court of the University of Hong Kong, of the St John's Cathedral Council, of St

---

10. This is the suggested translation of current staff and some alumni at SPC. The description 'young' probably refers to his being the younger Stewart brother.

11. In a postscript added to A. Stewart, After Seventy Years, 21.

12. E. Stewart, Hong Kong Volunteers, Appendix VIII, entry by Ride.

John's College Council, and of the Government's Appeal Board. Alongside all these responsibilities, Evan's most regular commitment was attending St John's Cathedral week by week and serving as a sidesman, humbly helping parishioners and visitors to find a seat and feel at home.

In early 1953 Evan received another honor. He was invited to the whole Hong Kong contingent in Queen Elizabeth II's Coronation Procession on 2 June. Ten days before the event, he joined four hundred representatives from other British colonies, who were accommodated at the Royal Artillery Barracks in Woolwich. The first morning, all were inspected by Prince Philip, the Duke of Edinburgh. On 27 May there was a colorful Dress Rehearsal and, a day later, Evan and Dorothy attended the Queen's Garden Party at Buckingham Palace.

On the day of the Coronation, the service was broadcast from Westminster Abbey on loudspeakers to around three million spectators. At 1.30pm precisely, the lead Army band struck up and, according to Evan's first-hand account, in the rain "we moved out into Whitehall into a volume of cheering of which I have never heard the like . . . no people on earth can cheer like the Londoners." When the procession reached half way, it briefly halted "during which the Northern Rhodesians were mistaken by the crowd for Australians and serenaded with 'Waltzing Matilda.'" Later, after rounding Admiralty Arch, we marched "down the Mall with colours flying and swords at the carry in one final grand burst."[13] The five-mile-long parade took almost an hour to march past the crowds. Among these were Dorothy and Michael who had been allocated good seats in a stand near Park Lane. As Michael remembers: "It was a most impressive Procession and we were very proud of my father marching at the head of the Hong Kong detachment, knowing that marching with his 'dropped-foot' was painful."[14] This was the first coronation to be televised, and was watched by over twenty million people worldwide.

The following morning the troops assembled at Buckingham Palace and were inspected by the Queen, "who looked radiant and not in the least tired . . . and at the top of the steps took the salute." Evan concludes that it was a privilege to "have played a part, infinitesimal though it may have been, in the greatest, the most brilliant, and the most impressive Pageant that the world has yet seen." [15] It was not until three days later, after a visit to Evan's old regiment, the Middlesex, that he was officially off-duty. Evan and Dorothy were then able to catch up with Mildred and Reg in their new placement

13. Stewart, *Hong Kong Volunteers*, 2020, Appendix VII.
14. From Personal correspondence with Michael Stewart.
15. Stewart, *Hong Kong Volunteers*, 2020, Appendix VII.

at St John's Church, Epping. They also spent time with Arthur and Kitty in Bournemouth, where he had recently suffered a major stroke. Seeing him confined to bed and hardly able to speak was quite a shock. Having shared so much of their lives together, when it was time to say goodbye both of them found it difficult. Shortly after, Evan and Dorothy returned to Hong Kong, they received the half-expected news that Arthur had passed away. Evan was pleased that Michael could represent him at the funeral but was grateful for his last opportunity to spend time with his much-loved brother, friend, and mentor.

大屠殺中倖存的孩子們

Later that year, Harry Wittenbach, who after his release from Stanley became East Asia Secretary of CMS, undertook a three-month tour of the Society's work in the region. According to his report on Hong Kong:

> After the Communist Party came to power on the Mainland, the Chinese government generally left Hong Kong alone, rarely discussing even its political status. In spite of this,
> the life of the British Colony is largely dominated by China, just across the border. It is refugees from Communist China who have flooded the Colony, living in great houses on the Peak, or in the new blocks of flats in Kowloon, in the crowded tenement houses or in the shanty towns which have grown up on every hillside, swelling to over three million the population which normally is under one million . . . Communist aggression in Korea and Indochina, and threats to Malaya, Burma and Siam, have failed to arouse alarm in Hong Kong. Everywhere new buildings are being erected, hotels, business houses, residences. A vast new reservoir is nearing completion in the hills of the New Territories, to augment the overtaxed water supply. What is the reason for this confidence? . . . Hong Kong reckons on another forty years of life and anticipates no trouble during that time . . . From the point of view of Christian strategy, the task before us is to utilise these remaining years in building up in Hong Kong churches and Christian leadership that will endure.[16]

Turning to the Colleges in Hong Kong, he noted that at St Stephen's, from which Ernest Martin was just retiring as Principal: "There are 250 boys

---

16. This was H. A. Wittenbach in 'Tour of East Asia 1953–1954', *East Asia General*, 20–22

in the College of whom 130 are boarders, 177 in the Prep. School, of whom 120 are boarders, and 24 boys and girls in the new kindergarten. St Stephen's has refused to accept any government grants and that necessitates the charging of high fees.[17] Up to the present, the demand for education has been so great that this has been no obstacle." At St Paul's, "Evan Stewart is blessed with a thoroughly loyal staff of experienced teachers. His forty year's service has made him almost a legend and his distinguished war service a hero. He is probably one of the best-loved people in Hong Kong. He works far too hard and his wife would like him to retire at the end of this tour of service; but, unless some suitable work were found for him in England, Evan would never be happy . . . There are 500 students in 13 classes. The new block of classrooms is a magnificent building." [18]

Evan and Dorothy at St Paul's Sports Day, 1954

Under Evan's leadership, all aspects of SPC continued to develop. After St Paul's opened at Bonham Road, good sportsmen continued to emerge, some becoming well-known in the Colony. With Evan's support, the 10th Scouts became better equipped and a Senior Scout Group developed.

17. After three years in a parish in the UK, Ernest returned to the Colony and became Acting-Warden at St John's Hall at the Hong Kong University. As College Chaplain from 1956 till his retirement in 1980, he was deeply appreciated for his care of students, and more highly regarded than the Master of St John's. In 1978, Ernest received a Member of the British Empire award for his educational and welfare services to Hong Kong. He died on 6 May 1981.

18. 'Tour of East Asia', *East Asia General*, 22 and 25 respectively.

Winning the Prince of Wales Banner Competition in 1953, the 10th was renamed the Governor's Group. The Christian Union had around fifty regular members, and held two annual camps, one at Stanley, and its Chairman, Peter Kwong, was to became the first Chinese Archbishop of the Hong Kong Sheng Kung Hui Church. The Old Boys reformed themselves as the St Paul's College Alumni Association. Its Committee consisted of many well-known people in Hong Kong and considerably expanded its activities. Academically, the number of students who passed the Certificate of Education Examinations was the highest in Hong Kong. To double the capacity of its future student intake, Evan also developed "a master plan to utilize the site to build new and up-to-date buildings in stages."[19]

On New Year's Day 1955, Evan was awarded another prestigious honor, 'Officer of the Order of the British Empire'. The Citation commended him for "40 years continuous service as a Volunteer, including active service in two wars in both of which he was wounded. His record both in war and in peace is outstanding", especially his "sterling qualities of inspired leadership and devotion to duty . . . His record has been a brilliant example, to more than one generation in this Colony, of unselfish and invaluable public service."[20] The award was presented by the Governor of Hong Kong in the presence of other dignitaries at Government House. The next year Evan was made Honorary Colonel of the Hong Kong Regiment. He "placed this appointment above all honours and it was a source of great pleasure to him that he was able to serve on to the last."[21] Unfortunately, later that same year Evan suffered a stroke. Being unable to walk even a short distance was now very difficult. Although often in pain, he was always in good spirits and remained as enthusiastic as ever.

The following year, Evan received a letter from Reg in Lewes, on the south coast near Brighton, that his dear sister Mil, aged seventy-five, had suffered a stroke and passed away. His mind ranged over the years the two of them had shared together in Aunt Tem's house, and how she had been a kind of second mother to him. In October 1958, Evan suffered another stroke and was hospitalized in Queen Mary Hospital. One of his close military colleagues recorded: "I had the pleasure of visiting the Home Guard in camp and I promised them I would give their former Commanding Officer their best wishes. By this time Evan could neither speak nor make any signs, but mentally he was still very active and as I mentioned each name, his face

---

19. Fung, *From Devotion to Plurality*, 90.
20. This citation was provided courtesy of Michael Stewart.
21. Stewart, *Hong Kong Volunteers*, 2020, Appendix VIII, entry by Lindsay Ride.

would light up with what was left of that smile we all knew so well . . ."[22] His death from a major stroke on Wednesday 17 December was highlighted in the following morning's edition of the *South China Morning Post*. First, there was a private funeral, for which Michael flew out from the UK, then, on Tuesday 23 December, a Memorial Service at the Cathedral attended by staff, past and present students, military personnel, and scouts.

Evan Stewart DSO, OBE, ED

Among the tributes that flowed from his passing were:

"We are told that one of his earliest memories was the murder of his parents and a brother and sister. He met this challenge by returning to devote his life to the service of those same people against whom a lesser man might well have nursed a grievance."[23]

"Evan didn't do things in order to be thanked and he shunned all suggestions of personal publicity and individual demonstrations of every kind, but his main objection would be on the score of the trouble it would be to others. Thoughtfulness and concern for others were one of his very main qualities . . . Evan would never shirk a job that needed doing, especially if it

22. Stewart, *Hong Kong Volunteers*, 2020, Appendix VIII, entry by Lindsay Ride.

23. From an obituary by Colonel H. Owen-Hughes, *St John's Review*, February 1959, 42.

involved even the merest suggestion of duty, or of help to others, or of help to a cause."[24]

"Evan Stewart commended his own firm faith to his students by his strong Christian life and character . . . never had one of our colleagues in CMS received such proof of honour and affection as shown at the great Service of Thanksgiving."[25]

"What shall be our concise picture of Evan Stewart? First, that he has been led by a guiding principle and has understood his task. Second, that nothing may deflect him from the path of his principles. Third, that his task shall be fulfilled. . ... To me he will always be the embodiment of the 'Happy Warrior', the modern crusader wearing the whole armour of God who leaves us with the motto of those warriors of old 'Be Steadfast, Brave and True.'"[26]

"A teacher above all things, even as Headmaster, he did more teaching himself than the pundits say a Headmaster properly should. The result is that he never had to give orders. His own example of doing more than he should has been infectious so that his staff have willingly followed his example."[27]

"His lifetime of service is a fine example and witness to his faith . . . He was essentially a kind man who never bore malice or spoke unkindly of anyone. [He] will be greatly missed by the boys and staff of St Paul's College, and a very large number of people in Hong Kong, and the United Kingdom."[28]

"Now Evan has gone where so many of his men of No. 3 Company were waiting to greet him. Those of us who remain are better and happier for having known him. One by one we shall no doubt rejoin the ranks, and Evan will be there, in his easy happy way, gallantly sending us on into that receding, ever-widening tapestry."[29]

Let Ernest have the last word:

"He was a very inspiring teacher, even to the present year when he helped his boys to gain excellent results . . . [despite his disability] he was a man of great endurance and strong physique . . . no one would deny him his charm or Irish wit, his modesty, or his courage. A regular worshipper at church, he expressed his convictions in his life. He is one of those who will be remembered because beloved. He had his faults, those of a certain

---

24. E. Stewart, Hing Kong Volunteers, Appendix VIII, entry by Lindsay Ride.
25. Missionaries' Committee of CMS Hong Kong, January 1959.
26. Owen-Hughes in *St John's Review*, February 1959, 42–43, slightly re-ordered.
27. Bishop R. O. Hall in *St John's Review*, February 1959, 42.
28. Minute of the Executive Committee, 21 January 1959 signed by Max Warren, CMS General Secretary.
29. Stewart, *Hong Kong Volunteers*, 2020, Appendix VIII, entry by Bevan Field.

carelessness (never indulged in any military matter) . . . laughable and loveable, calling for immediate aid from those nearest him, who never failed him . . . One of the reasons that he was beloved by many, was that he was never heard to express any unkind criticism of anyone. For his wife and son we pray continued courage, remembering John Bunyan's words that when he passed over "All the trumpets were sounding for him on the other side."[30]

Memorial Service at SPC for Evan

The ashes of the last survivor of the Hwasang massacre were buried under the College where he had served for forty-five years.

大屠殺中倖存的孩子們

Since Evan's death, his son Michael has become the guardian of the Stewart family history. Recently he shared a remarkable story of memorabilia that survived the massacre at Hwasang.

> When he was killed, my grandfather had with him a metal deed box. The "Vegetarians" thought it must contain money and so hacked it open with an axe, but were disappointed when they found it only contained papers and threw it away. A few weeks

---

30. E. Martin in *St John's Review*, February 1959, 41. This also appeared in the *South China Morning Post*, 24 December 1958, 7.

later, other missionaries were looking through the ashes of the burnt-out house and found the remains of the box. They took the jagged lid, engraved with the Stewart crest and family motto 'Forward', and sent it to the CMS office in London. Over the years it passed through several hands and was eventually given to me.[31]

Like their parents before them, the Stewart children saw "Forward" as a motto for their lives as well.[32] They were committed to laying a foundation for individuals and institutions in China, that would endure well into the future, pass into the hands of local leadership, and give rise to fresh initiatives. Their lives modeled the cost and sacrifice needed to bring this about. The following profiles illustrate something of their remarkable 'forward' influence on individuals.

Wong Shiu Pun (Preston) was born in Hong Kong in 1890. Preston studied psychology and theology at Queen's College, Cambridge. In 1912, he began teaching at SPC. Through Arthur's influence, he became a Christian and was appointed the first Housemaster in the College. He was a key leader in the 10th Hong Kong (St Paul's) Scout Group and established SPC's Day School program. Preston became a member of the Police Reserve, and in the late 1930s joined an anti-Japanese resistance group based in Police, Scout, and Chinese Christian circles. During the Occupation, he was recruited by the BAAG to provide intelligence about enemy troop and ship movements. In May 1943, along with several others, he was arrested and interned in Stanley Prison. At his trial, Preston was sentenced to death, but for several months awaited this in solitary confinement. Then, on 29 October, thirty-two men and one woman were taken to Stanley beach, blindfolded, and in groups of three executed. Preston was allowed to say prayers for the group, asked for the forgiveness of the killers, and was the last to be beheaded. He is remembered today by the Wong Shui Pun Prize for Religious Education at SPC, as well as by a similar Community Service Award named after his wife, Phyllis, who continued as Evan's secretary at the College for many years. According to Arthur: "I have never known a Chinese who has meant more to me than him."[33]

---

31. From private correspondence with Michael Stewart.

32. Appropriately, the first account of Robert, Louisa, and their six children's service in China, was a sixteen-page booklet by H. A.Wittenbach, 'Forward': The motto and challenge of the Stewart family of Hwasang, Fukien" published in 1948.

33. A. Stewart, After Seventy Years, 15. On Wong Shuu Puu, see further *The Dark World's Fire*.

James C. Y. Yen in China

Yen Yang-chu (James) was born in Szechwan in 1893. Yen was educated at a missionary school where he was converted to Christianity. A few years later, James Stewart invited him to become his Chinese assistant at the newly established University Hostel in Chengtu, and later encouraged him to prepare at SSC for University. After James' death in 1916, Yen adopted his English name because "Jim Stewart inspired in me the crusading spirit and missionary zeal . . . I am eternally indebted to him."[34] Towards the end of WW1, Yen worked with the YMCA in France among the largely uneducated Chinese Labour Corps. This experience led him to create a Literacy Primer, using just over a thousand basic characters, that opened up ordinary people's first opportunity to read and write. He did this by translating Chinese classics, folktales, songs, as well as information about farming methods, hygiene, and even democracy. After undergraduate study at Yale and postgraduate study at Princeton, where he was President of the Christian Student Association, Yen formed the Mass Education Movement, made up of volunteer teachers and local leaders, which reached millions of illiterate Chinese. Following its success, Yen founded the Rural Reconstruction Movement, a grassroots effort to create a nation that did not depend on foreign funding, government control, or violent revolution. In May 1943, he

---

34. *Church Missionary Gleaner*, 2 February 1920, no page.

was one of ten 'modern revolutionaries'—including Albert Einstein, Henry Ford, Walt Disney, and John Dewey—to receive the prestigious Copernican award. His work in China was interrupted by the Japanese invasion, held up by the Civil war, and finally halted by the Communist victory. In the US, Yen then founded the International Institute of Rural Reconstruction, a movement that currently operates in more than 50 countries around the world. In 1990, the Association of James Yen was established in Beijing and published more than ten volumes of his writings. In 2001 China Central TV broadcast a nationwide program on him in its series of outstanding Chinese leaders. Y. C. Yen's basic commitment was to what he called the three "C's"– Christ, Chinese culture, and ordinary Citizens. He saw himself as a missionary of the gospel of 'Hope and Release' for the peasants of his own country. Yen agreed with the words of Sun Yat-sen that "Our greatest hope is to make the Bible and Christian education, as we have known it, the means of conveying to our countrymen what blessings may be in the way of just laws." [35]

Choy Wai-chuen was born in Hong Kong in 1914 and studied at SSC from the mid-20s to the early 30s. As well as being one of his teachers, Kathleen taught him to play tennis, a game she had enjoyed since her youth in Ireland. Choy's talent soon became obvious, and after professional coaching, he began playing competitively in Hong Kong. After gaining his degree from Cambridge University, as well as a 'Half Blue' for his sporting achievement, he was selected for the first Chinese Davis Cup team. Choy then competed each year in Grand Slams at Wimbledon, and in 1938 reached the third round. In the same year, he also played in the quarter-finals of the British Hardcourt Championships. At that time, he was deeply sceptical of the British PM's pact with Hitler, declaring it as worse than a treaty with the Devil! Concerned for the starving millions in war-torn China, Wai-chuen played in Exhibition matches in the US that raised funds to alleviate their suffering. Then, as a Goodwill Ambassador for the United China Relief, he organized a team to do the same in China. In November 1941, for its first tournament at Hong Kong's Chinese Recreation Club, he arranged special seats so Kathleen could be his guest of honor. According to a US team-mate and friend, "He was a Chinese gentleman in every sense of the word . . . a brilliant scholar . . . spoke English perfectly . . . with a magnetic personality." [36] Influenced by the teaching and example he had received at SSC, Choy

---

35. Sharman, *Sun Yat-sen*, 310. Among several books on Yen's life and work, see Hayford, *To the People*. Through Yen's influence, The Rev James R. Stewart Memorial Fellowship was established "with the hope and prayer that many young missionaries, men and women, may catch his spirit and follow his Christ-like example." The Fellowship was initially administered by Ernest Martin and the Bishop of Hong Kong.

36. Harman, *Hellions of Hirohito*, ch.1.

believed that more than anything else China needed a program of education built on the centrality of love and unselfishness. Having escaped to Macau after the Japanese invasion of Hong Kong, he tried unsuccessfully to arrange the rescue of a team-mate in the Stanley Internment Camp. After the war, Choy continued to compete in tennis competitions, winning a couple of national titles, until his early death in London from leukemia in 1951.

Bishop and Mrs Song

Song Cheng-Tsi was born in Szechwan in 1890. Song was one of the earliest graduates of West China Christian Union University. Though James Stewart became his mentor, it was Reg Taylor who baptized Song in 1916 after family hostility to his conversion had died down. Mildred befriended Mrs Song, frequently offered hospitality, and helped guide her as a young mother. After theological training at both Wycliffe Hall, Oxford, and Ridley College, Cambridge, C. T. Song was ordained in the Anglican Church. Eventually, he and his wife had a large family of seven children. In 1929, Song was chosen by Dr Howard Mowll as his Assistant Bishop of West China, the first Chinese to serve in that position. He had remarkable influence with students, attracting hundreds of school students to a Bible Class on Sundays, and broadcasting the Christian message weekly to a wide audience. Three years later he was asked to be Chair of the Convocation and Board of Directors at the University and Visiting Professor in Religious Studies there. In the following years, violent bandit activity and rival military struggles sometimes made traveling round the Diocese risky, but Song continued to carry out his pastoral responsibilities. In 1939 he was elected Bishop of West China. His concern for the wider community so deeply impressed City authorities, that they declared the church as no longer a foreign organization with a foreign leader! In 1943, he was invited by Bishop R. O. Hall to make an extended visit to Hong Kong, during which time his own house and church in Chengdu were bombed, though fortunately his family was unhurt. Song was also invited by Archbishop Mowll to make the first of two visits to Australia, where he spoke at civic events, universities, and theological colleges, as well as met with business, professional and political leaders. By the end of the war, prolonged strain and overwork led to his handing over some responsibilities and focussing his discretionary time on university teaching and student ministry. He was regarded by Bishop Hall as the "outstanding Szechwanese leader"[37], who combined traditional Chinese learning with a deep Christian faith. Although coming from the landlord class, and a church leader, he was not imprisoned when the Communists came to power. On 15 August 1950, he resigned, dying from a stroke five years later.

大屠殺中倖存的孩子們

The Stewart children also had a significant 'forward' influence on the institutions they founded or served.

St Paul's College describes the period when Arthur and Evan were Principals, between 1909 and 1958, as its "Golden Years". Today it continues as one of the leading schools in Hong Kong. Enrolments currently stand at around 1200 secondary and 600 primary students. The College seeks to offer education in line with 'Evangelical, Protestant, and Christian principles.' The school motto is "The fear of the Lord is the beginning of wisdom" (Psalm 9:10) and *We Build Our School on Thee, O Lord* is the college hymn. The Christian Union continues to meet regularly and is involved in various off-campus ministries. Students are encouraged to participate in community services through such organizations as the Youth Red Cross, Scout Group, and Community Youth Club, as well as charitable work with those who are disabled and in aged care. Its graduates have occupied such influential positions as the first Chinese member of the Hong Kong Legislative Council; Judge of the Court of International Justice in the Hague; founder of the S. K. Yee Medical Foundation and of the Chinese Bank; Archbishop and Primate of the Hong Kong Sheng Kung Hui; Chair Professor in Electoral

---

37. Bishop Hall in Yuang, *Streams of Living Water*, 8.

Engineering in Imperial College London, and Educational Inspector of Schools of Singapore. Others have devoted their lives to ministry in the church in Taiwan, Australia, Canada, and elsewhere.[38]

St. Paul's Girls (now Co-Educational) College was founded in 1915. "Faith, Hope, and Love" (1 Corinthians 13:13) continues to be its motto. The goal is to develop students as whole people on the basis of the Christian faith, making no distinction on family or social background. It strives to instill attitudes and values that form a sense of responsibility to the community and society. Currently, there are around 1,200 students. Highly regarded for its focus and expertise in music, its choir and orchestras are often called upon to perform at public events and venues. Graduates have become teachers, nurses, writers, lawyers, and doctors in Hong Kong, Taiwan, China, and other Asian countries, often occupying high-level positions.

St Stephen's College is the largest secondary college, and one of the few boarding schools, in Hong Kong. It ranks within the top ten percent of schools in the Territory. As Headmaster and wife, Ernest and Kathleen played a prominent leadership role for twenty-five years. Now co-educational, enrolments are around 1200 students. Many of its buildings are listed as Historic Monuments, and it was the first campus to set up a Heritage Trail, showcasing documents, photographs, and sites connected with both its Christian origins and the Stanley Internment Camp. After the war, a Chapel was built to commemorate those who died during the Japanese Occupation. "Faith is the foundation of knowledge" remains the College motto, and it continues to provide a caring and supportive Christian environment for the "moral, intellectual, physical, social, aesthetic and spiritual development" of its students. Philip established its reputation for the medical care of its boarders. Students are divided into six houses, one named after Arthur, and another after Ernest. Distinguished alumni have included the first Chief Executive of the Hong Kong Special Administrative Region; Vice-President of the Olympic Council of Asia; Chairman of the Canton Trust and Commercial Bank; Chairlady of People's Power, and several members of the Legislative and Executive Councils. St Stephen's Preparatory School, founded by Kathleen, is an important conduit to St Stephen's College and has grown to 600 students.

St Stephen's Girls College had Kathleen as the first member of staff alongside its founding Headmistress. Still under the auspices of the Hong Kong Sheng Kung Hui Church, its motto is "Faith To Go Forward", and "We build our school O Lord on Thee" is its College hymn. It strives to educate

---

38. As noted earlier, the story of SPS until 2000 may be found in Fung, *From Devotion to Plurality*.

the whole person, equipping young women to fulfill their potential and serve God through serving others, their communities, and society. With the Chaplain's assistance, there are student-led morning assemblies including prayers, hymns, and Bible readings, as well as regular Christian Fellowship and Bible Study groups, and an annual Summer Camp. The College presently has around 1100 students, ranks eighth among all secondary schools in Hong Kong, and has produced ten winners of the Territory's Outstanding Student Awards. It was among the first to send girls to the University of Hong Kong, with others studying since at Cambridge, Oxford, MIT, Yale, and the Julliard School of Music, and a number progressing to the top echelons of politics, academia, church, media and the arts in Hong Kong.[39]

West China Christian Union (now Sichuan) University was the venue for the CMS Student Hostel established by James, and where he also taught some classes. It was soon extended by him to include a chapel, reading room, and staff residences, becoming in effect a small College, in which Reg and Mildred also worked. When Archbishop Mowll passed through Chengdu in 1946, he found the CMS College that developed from the Hostel "filled to capacity" with students coming from "various places" in China.[40] After 1950, this institution, and a few specialty institutes, gradually developed into what is now known as Sichuan University. Helped by the influx of academics during the Japanese invasion, this became one of China's top universities. Its current student body has nearly 40,000 undergraduate and 20,000 postgraduate students, including many from overseas. The University is one of a small number in China that has an Institute of Religious Studies, which includes an interest in the study of Christianity.

大屠殺中倖存的孩子們

The Stewart family motto and influence continued to shape the life and work of the next generation, as the following bios show:

Robert Michael Stewart was born in Hong Kong. Michael was Evan and Dorothy's only child. After graduating from University College of the University of London, he worked for thirty years at Imperial Chemical Industries, and was General Manager of Phillips Imperial Petroleum. Like his father, he also had an an army connection, first with the Royal Signals, later as Commanding Officer of a TA Regiment, a Colonel Commandant and Honorary Colonel. Over the years, Michael's concern for the young,

---

39. The story of the College until 1995 is told in Barker, *Change and Continuity*.
40. Mowll, *Memorable Nine Weeks*, 19.

education, and welfare expressed itself in serving on the Boards of Children's Charities, Youth Development Programmes, and Community Ventures. A honor bestowed on him was to e made an Aide-de-Camp to Her Majesty Queen Elizabeth II from 1975–1980, and High Sheriff of Cleveland from 1990–1991. For his various services, like Evan, he was awarded the Officer of the Order of the British Empire. Throughout his life, Michael has sought to reflect the strong Christian convictions his parents taught and lived. In 2008 he was invited by the Alumni Association of SPC as Guest of Honor at the 50th anniversary of his father's death. Now in his nineties, he lives in the north-east of England.

Margaret Ride was born in Hong Kong, the older daughter of Arthur and Kitty. A trained kindergarten teacher, she returned to Hong Kong in 1947 and taught at St Stephen's Girl School. In 1951 she married David Ride, the son of Sir Lindsay Tasman Ride, in Hong Kong. After a short time in Oxford, where Margaret continued teaching, David was appointed Director of the Western Australian Museum in Perth. There she gave herself mainly to raising five children but, when her first child reached school-age, taught Scripture at a local primary school, and Sunday School at her local church. Some years later they moved to Canberra, where David became Principal of the College of Advanced Education. For the rest of her life, Margaret was deeply involved in church life, as a chorister, elder, Sunday school superintendent, and ran a weekly Friendship group. Her community activities included serving with Meals on Wheels and helping with Riding for the Disabled. In 1984 Margaret was present at David's award of Member of the Order of Australia for his service to Science and Education. Together with David, she hosted a weekly Home Fellowship Group. Margaret outlived her husband and died in 2019, aged 94.

Lionel Robert Stewart Taylor, Mildred and Reg's only son, was born in Szechwan. After graduating from Emmanuel College, Cambridge, and St Thomas' Hospital, London, he became a Fellow of the Royal College of Surgeons. Joining the Royal Naval Volunteer Reserve in 1941, he served throughout the war as a Lieutenant Surgeon. A lover of sports, for many years he competed in the Monte Carlo and Royal Automobile Club. An eminent member of the medical profession, Lionel's last appointment was as Senior Surgeon to the ENT Department of Charing Cross Hospital. Around the same time, his sister Kathleen rose to the position of Senior Physiotherapist at Stoke Mandeville Orthopaedic Hospital, where her uncle Evan had earlier been a patient. In 1971, Lionel was invited by the Old Boys of Trinity College Foochow, in Singapore to speak at an important anniversary of the institution founded by his grandfather and namesake. According to the British Medical Journal, "He was a practising Christian who lived by his beliefs, strongly supporting his local parish church, and quietly instrumental in obtaining financial support for both ecclesiastical and medical charities. A true gentleman, kindly in manner, tolerant in adversity, but firm in his principles, his gentleness was reflected in his surgery . . . and in his attention to detail."[41] After a short illness, Lionel died, aged only fifty-seven, in 1972.

Joan Mosley was born in Hong Kong in 1929, the younger daughter of Arthur and Kitty. Mainly raised in England, in 1954 she married William, a banker with the Hong Kong and Shanghai Banking Corporation in Singapore. In 1962, she went with him to Hong Kong, where they lived for the next thirteen years. Along with being a committed member of the Red Cross, Joan was strongly involved in the worship and work of St John's Cathedral, with a particular focus on the needs of the many drug addicts in Hong Kong. After returning to England in 1975, she led a CMS group and had a special concern for an Orphanage in Uganda, which she also visited. In 1985, Joan and other members of the family attended the centennial of a stained-glass window of Louisa Stewart in Liverpool Cathedral. One of her sons is the well-known British television presenter and medical journalist, Dr Michael Mosley.

---

41. From the Obituary Notices, *British Medical Journal*, 2 December, 1972, 555.

Epilogue

WHEN ROBERT AND LOUISA Stewart married and left for China, they had no idea what the future held for them, only the promise "I will be with you always . . . ."[1] In August 1895, it looked like their work had come to a dramatic end, and within a generation be forgotten. What the couple didn't know was that their children would carry on the vision, and take it to levels they could never have imagined.

Though each of the surviving Stewarts had distinct personalities, abilities and interests, they all believed there was still "unfinished business in China". Like Robert and Louisa, they came to realise that education was the main strategy, not only for reaching people with the gospel, but for preparing them to make a difference to their society. The suffering they had experienced through losing their parents, brother and sister, gave them a great capacity to empathise with people in need, and a desire to protect those who were vulnerable. None of them ever forgot that they had grown up as orphans. Though independent of mind, all were collaborative in spirit. Despite the physical and psychological challenges involved, they were willing to take risks for the sake of others. The Stewarts felt at home in Chinese culture, befriended, relied on and learned from local people, so much so that they did not ever really want to leave. Though circumstances prevented some from remaining, two children of the massacre still lie in Chinese soil on either side of Hong Kong Island.

More than seventy-five years ago, Bishop Hall declared that "someday the full story of the Stewart family must be written,"[2] and it has been our privilege to share their lives for a time and attempt just that. The whole Stewart family was inexorably tied to China in life and death, and through both brought faith, hope, and love to what will one day be the most powerful and influential country in the world.

1. Matthew 28:20 ASV.
2. From a document courtesy of Michael Stewart.

Appendix
Australian Connections with the Stewart Family

THERE WERE SEVERAL KINDS of connections between the Stewarts and Australia over the five decades between 1890 and 1950.

* *Personal visits by the Stewarts to Australia itself.* The first of these was Robert's speaking tour of NSW and Victoria in the 1890s. A decade later, James spent two years studying in Sydney and, at the start of the Great War, enlisted in the Australian Chaplains Corps. Arthur and Kitty visited Sydney and Melbourne in the early 1920s. Dorothy and her son Michael's evacuation to New South Wales took place just before the Japanese invasion of Hong Kong. After the war, Evan passed through Sydney en route to England, and soon after this Arthur made a return visit. Following her time teaching in Hong Kong, his daughter, Margaret, married the Australian David Ride, and spent the rest of her life in various parts of the country.

* *Direct consequences of these visits for Australian missionary work in China.* Robert's trip in 1892 led to the development of the Church Missionary Association in two Australian states. The Saunders sisters from Melbourne were called to China through his ministry, and joined the Stewarts in Kucheng, as did Annie Gordon from Queensland, all three being massacred in Hwasang. After the sisters' death, their mother, Eliza went to Fukien and served there until she died. Two members of our own wider family, Sophie Newton and Amy Oxley, also went to Fukien as a result of hearing Robert speak. Later, several other Australian women were challenged by the Hwasang massacre to train for missionary work in China.

* *Regular contact between the Stewarts and Australian missionaries.* In Szechwan, Mildred spent time with a new CMS colleague, Victoria Mannett, while she was teaching at Mienchuh. Victoria also traveled with her and James up the Yangtze to Shanghai before the Nationalist Revolution. Mildred and Reg got to know Bishop Howard, and Dorothy, Mowll, who later moved to Australia to become Archbishop of Sydney and Anglican

Primate of Australia. In Hong Kong, Arthur, Kathleen, and later Evan were in regular contact with Rev E. Judd Barnett, from Victoria, who for a time was Warden at St Stephen's College, and later Archdeacon in the Diocese of South China.

* *Some of the Stewarts' activities left a tangible legacy in Australia.* James' link with the Australian Chaplains Corps in 1915 led to his name being included in the Roll of Honour of both the University of Sydney and the Australian War Memorial. Arthur's visit in the early 1920s resulted in Paul T'so, one of his early converts, moving to Melbourne to lead the Chinese Mission there for several years. During Archbishop Howard Mowll's time, a stained-glass memorial window was dedicated in Sydney's St Andrew's Cathedral, depicting James Stewart' teaching students in Chengdu, among them the future Bishop Song. In 1942 Song himself made a highly public and effective extended speaking tour of universities and churches in Australia.

* *Some Stewarts relied closely for a limited time on specific Australian CMS workers.* Arthur developed a strong link with Gertrude Bendelack, from Melbourne, who was Principal of St Hilda's Girls School, Canton. As well as working together on an Education Committee over the years, during unrest in Canton he invited her to teach at St Paul's, and for a time to act as his Deputy Principal. Jack and Mary Asche, from Victoria, joined St Stephen's staff in the mid-20s and helped Ernest rebuild the College after the War. When NSW missionary Norah Dillon's work in Canton was halted by Japanese aggression, Kathleen invited her to take charge for a year of the new St Stephen's Preparatory School.

There were other less significant links between the Stewarts and Australia. For example, several other CMS missionaries were recruited to the staff of St Paul's and St Stephen's Colleges. Links were formed in Hong Kong with Australians like Dr Lindsay Ride through mutual involvement in the Hong Kong Volunteer Defence Corps. After WW2, an official visit to Hong Kong, Szechwan, and Fukien was made by Archbishop Howard and Dorothy Mowll.

Bibliography

Anglican Church of Canada. www.anglican.ca.
Anslow, Barbara. "Memories of Life in Old Hong Kong." guolo.com>node/.
Archer, Bernice, and Kent Fedorovich. "The Women of Stanley: Internment in Hong Kong 1942–45." *Women's History Review* 5:3, 19 December 2006. At https://doi.org/10.1080/09612029600200119/.
Banham, Tony. "Evacuation of British Women and Children from Hong Kong to Australia in 1940." PhD thesis in the School of Humanities and Social Sciences, University of New South Wales, Sydney, 2008.
———. *Not the Slightest Chance: The Defence of Hong Kong, 1941*. Vancouver: University of British Columbia, 2003.
———, *We Shall Suffer There: Hong Kong's Defenders Imprisoned, 1942–1945*. Hong Kong: University of Hong Kong Press, 2009.
———. *The Sinking of the Lisbon Maru: Britain's Forgotten War Tragedy*. Hong Kong: Hong Kong University Press, 2010.
Banks, Linda, and Robert Banks. *View from the Faraway Pagoda: An Australian Pioneer Missionary in China from the Boxer Uprising to the Communist Insurgency*. Melbourne: Acorn, 2012.
———. *"They Shall See His Face": The Story of Amy Oxley Wilkinson and Her Visionary Blind School in China*. Studies in Chinese Christianity. Eugene, OR: Wipf & Stock, 2020.
Banks, Robert. "The Influence of the Keswick Movement on Missionary Work in China, 1880–1920." *Lucas*, Series 2, 9, 2015–2016, 49–72.
Barker, Kathleen. E. *Change and Continuity: A History of St Stephen's Girls College Hong Kong, 1906–1996*. Hong Kong: St Stephen's College, 1996.
Barnes I. H. *Behind the Great Wall: The Story of CEZMS Work and Workers in China*. London: Marshall, 1896.
Berry, D. M. *The Sister Martyrs of Kucheng: Letters and Memoirs of the Saunders Sisters in Foochow*. London: Nisbet, 1895.
"Beyond 1914: The University of Sydney and the Great War." James Robert Stewart. https://www.heuristplus.sydney.edu.au.
Boreham, F. W. "The C.M.S. in the Union University and Middle School, Chengtu." *Bulletin of the Diocese of Western China* 118 October 1931, 25–30.
Bunbury, Turtle. *Easter Dawn—The 1916 Rising*. Macon, GA: Mercer University Press, 2015.

"Calamatous Typhoon at Hong Kong, The." 18 September 1906, Hong Kong University Library, Hong Kong.

Carlson, Elswoth. C. *The Fukien Missionaries, 1847–1880*. Cambridge: Harvard University Asia Center, 1974.

Carpenter, J., et al. *Christian Higher Education: A Global Reconnaissance*. Grand Rapids: Eerdmans, 2014.

Carroll, John A. *A Concise History of Hong Kong*. London: Rowan & Littlefield, 2007.

———. *Edge of Empires: Chinese Elites and British Colonialism in Hong Kong*. Hong Kong: Hong Kong University Press, 2007.

Chan-Yueng, Moira M. W. *The Practical Prophet: Bishop Ronald O. Hall of Kong and His Legacies*. Hong Kong: Hong Kong University Press, 2015.

Cheeseman, Graham. "Training for Service: An Examination of Change and Development in the Bible College Movement in the UK, 1873–2002." PhD Queen's University, Faculty of Theology, Belfast, 2002.

Church Missionary Society Archives: *Annual Letters of Missionaries, Bulletin of the Diocese of Western China, Church Missionary Gleaner, Church Missionary Intelligencer, Church Missionary Outlook, Church Missionary Review, CMS Home Gazette, East Asia General Japan and China, Home News for India, China and the Colonies, Missionaries' Committee of Hong Kong, Précis Book, South China Mission Original Papers, West China Missionary News*. At Adam Matthews Digital Publications: https://www.amdigital.co.uk/primary-sources/church-missionary-society-archive/.31.

College History. St Paul's College. www.spc.edu.hk.

Comerford, Patrick. "The Dublin Family Who Became Missionary Martyrs in China." 2016. www.patrickcomerford.com

Cornish, Paul, *Machine Guns and the Great War*. South Yorkshire: Pen & Sword Military, 2009.

Dawson, E. C. *Missionary Heroines of the Cross*. London: Seeley Service, 1930.

Donaghue, Emma. *The Pull of The Stars*. New York: Little, Brown, 2020.

"The Easter Rising: When Ireland Went to War." History Extra. At https://www.historyextra.com/.

"Easter Rising." In *The Collected Poems of William Butler Yeats*. 2nd rev. ed. New York: Scribner, 1996.

Emerson, Geoffrey C. *Hong Kong Internment, 1942–1945: Life in the Japanese Civilian Camp at Stanley*. Hong Kong: Hong Kong University Press, 2008.

"Evacuation of the Wounded in World War 1." *The History Press*. At https://www.thehistorypress.co.uk/.

Fagg, Margaret. *Two Golden Lilies from the Empire of the Rising Sun*. London: Marshall, 1927.

Flaherty, E. O. "Teachers and the Role of Women in Irish Education in the 19th and 20th Century." 8 March 2017. endaoflaherty.com/.

Fung, Vincent H. Y., ed. *From Devotion to Plurality: A Full History of St Paul's College 1851–2001*. Hong Kong: St Paul's College, 2011.

Global China Center. *Biographical Dictionary of Chinese Christianity*. www.bdcconline.net.

Graves, Robert. *Goodbye to All That*. London: Anchor, 1958.

Gwynn, R. M., E. M. Norton, B. W. Simpson. *"T. C. D. in China": A History of the Dublin University Fukien Mission 1885–1935*. Dublin: DUFM, 1936.

Hall, R.O. "Account of the Confirmation and Ordination of Dr T. C. Chao Sunday, 20th July, 1941." Sheng Kung Hui Documents, Bishop's House. Hong Kong.

Harman Phillip. *Hellions of Hirohito: A Factual Story of an American Youth's Torture and Imprisonment by the Japanese.* Los Angeles: DeVorss, 1944.

Hayford, Charles W. *To the People: James Yen and Village China.* New York: Columbia University Press, 1990.

Heritage Impact Assessment Report. Redevelopment of St Paul's Co-educational College (Phase 2), February 2011. Prepared by China. Prepared by China Point Consultants Ltd. www.amo.gov.hk.

"Hong Kong Resistance: The British Army Aid Group 1942–45." www.arcgis.com/.

Hopkins, Evan. *Thoughts on Life and Godliness.* Gloucester: Facsimile, 2016.

Horrocks, Robert James. "The Guangzhou-Hongkong Strike, 1925–1926: Hongkong Workers in an Anti-Imperialist Movement." PhD thesis, University of Leeds, 1994. www.etheses.whiterose.ac.uk/1947/.

Houghton, Frank. *Amy Carmichael of Dohnavur.* London: SPCK, 1953.

Hsu, Immanuel C. Y. *The Rise of Modern China.* 5th ed. New York: Oxford University Press, 1995.

Huang, Y. Y. *Streams of Life: On the Anniversary of the Martyrdom of Rev and Mrs Stewart and Their Colleagues, Fukien, China.* Singapore: Diocese of Singapore, 1972.

Kerr, Gordon. *A Short History of China: From Ancient Dynasties to Economic Powerhouse.* Harpenden: Oldcastle, 2013.

Killeen, Richard. *A Short History of Modern Ireland.* Kingston ON: McGill–Queens Uni-versity Press, 2004.

Kua, Philip. *Scouting in Hong Kong, 1910–2010.* Hong Kong: Scout Association of Hong Kong, 2011.

Lary, Diana. *China's Republic.* Cambridge: Cambridge University Press. 2007.

———. *The Chinese People at War: Human Suffering and Social Transformation 1937–1945.* Cambridge: Cambridge University Press, 2010.

Leck, Greg. *Captives of Empire: The Japanese Internments of Allied Civilians in China 1941–1945.* Philadelphia: Shandy, 2006.

Leung, Kwong-Hon. "The Impact of Mission Schools in Hong Kong (1842 -1905) on Traditional Chinese Education: A Comparative Study." Phd diss., Institute of Education, University of London, 1987.

Lindsay, Oliver, and Jon R. Harris. *The Battle of Hong Kong, 1941–1945: Hostage to Fortune.* Kingston ON: McGill–Queen's University Press, 2005.

Loane, Marcus. L. *Archbishop Mowll: The Biography of Howard West Kilvinton Mowll. Archbishop of Sydney and Primate of Australia.* London: Hodder and Stoughton, 1960.

Lutz, Jessie G. *China and the Christian Colleges 1856–1960.* New York: Cornell University Press, 1971.

———. *Chinese Politics and Christian Missions: The Anti-Christian Movements of 1920–1928.* New York: Crossroad, 1988.

"Machine Gun." In *International Encyclopaedia of the First World War.* At https//:www.encyclopedia.1914–1918-online.net/.

MacIntosh, John A. *Anglican Evangelicalism in Sydney 1897 to 1953.* Eugene, OR: Wipf & Stock, 2018.

MacGillivray, D. *China Mission Year Book for 1911*. Shanghai: Christian Literature Society for China, 1911.

Mannett, Victoria. "Girl Students in Chengtu." *The Bulletin of the Diocese of Western China* 116 (April 1933) 8–10.

Matthews, Clifford, and Oswald Cheung. *Dispersal and Renewal: Hong Kong University during the War Years*. Hong Kong: Hong Kong University Press, 1998.

Merci, Franco David. *Legacy from the Hill: The Early Years of St John's College*. Hong Kong: St John's College Alumni Association, 2012.

Mowll, Howard K. *A Memorable Nine Weeks: Being an Account by The Most Rev H. W. K. Mowll, Archbishop of Sydney, of His Recent Visit to the Jubilee Celebrations of the West China Mission*. Sydney: Church Missionary Society, 1946.

———. "West China Seen through the Eyes of a Westerner." Ninth Morrison Lecture. *East Asian History* 34 (2007) 117–31.

Mulhall, Daniel. *A New Day Dawning: A Portrait of Ireland in 1900*. London: Collins, 2000.

Ng, Peter T. M. "The Rise and Development of Christian Higher Education in China." In *Christian Higher Education: A Global Reconnaissance*, J. Carpenter et al., Grand Rapids: Eerdmans, 2014, 68–69.

Obituary Notices, *British Medical Journal*, 2 December 1972, 555.

Paine, S. C. M. *The Sino-Japanese War of 1894–1895: Perceptions, Power and Primacy*. Cambridge: Cambridge University Press, 2002.

Paterson, Cicely. *Celebrate! 200 Years of Taking the Gospel to the World*. Sydney: Church Missionary Society, 1998.

Piggin, Stuart, and Robert D. Linder. *The Fountain of Public Prosperity: Evangelical Christians in Australian History 1740–1914*. Melbourne: Monash, 2018.

Pollock, John C. *The Cambridge Seven*. Leicester, UK: InterVarsity Press, 1962.

"Prospectus St Paul's College, 1914." In *Hong Kong Memory*. At https://www.hkmemory.hk/collections/education/about/index.html/.

Puckle, Leslie. "Memories of Stanley Internment Camp." Gwulo: Old Hong Kong. At gwulo.com>node.

RAMC Officers of the Malta Garrison. Philip Smyly Stewart. At https://www.maltaramc.com/ramcoff/s/stewartps.html, 2.

Ream, Bill. *Too Hot for Comfort: War Years in China 1938–1950*. London: Epworth, 1988.

Record Details for Evan George Stewart (Labour Corps). Archive:WO 372/19/53789. At https://www.forces-war-records.co.uk/records/19867185/second-lieutenant-evan-george-stewart-labour-corps/.

Rowland, Charles. G. *Long Night's Journey into Day: Prisoners of War in Hong Kong and Japan 1941–1945*. Waterloo, ON: Wilfred Laurier University Press, 2001.

Sandbach, Joseph. Imperial War Museum. Catalogue No. 4784, 9 November 1980.

Service, John B. *Golden Inches: The China Memoir of Grace Service*. Berkeley: University of California Press, 1993.

Shan, Patrick F. "Triumph after Catastrophe: Church, State and Society in Post-Boxer China, 1900–1937." *Peace and Conflict Studies* 16/2 (2009) 13–50. At https://nsuworks.nova.edu/pcs

Sharman, Lynn. *Sun Yat-sen: His Life and Its Message*. New York, 1934.

Smith, Carl T. *Chinese Christians Elites, Middlemen and Church in Hong Kong*. Hong Kong: Hong Kong University Press, 2005.

Smyly, Ellen. *Erin's Hope: Journal of the Smyly Homes*. Dublin, 1896.
Smyly, Vivienne. *The Early History of Mrs Smyly's Homes and Schools*. Privately published c. 1976.
Smyly, William. *An Irish Family in the East. South China Sunday Post-Herald*. February-March 1959.
Snow, Philip. *The Fall of Hong Kong: Britain, China, and the Japanese Occupation*. New Haven: Yale University Press, 2004.
Stacke, FitzM. H. *The Worcestershire Regiment in the Great War*. 2 vols. Uckfield; Naval and Military Academy, 2002.
Stericker, John. *A Tear for the Dragon*. London: Barker, 1958.
Stewart, Arthur. After Seventy Years: An Autobiography. - Arthur Dudley Stewart (1877–1953). 1947.
Stewart, Evan. *A Record of the Hong Kong Volunteers in Battle. December 1941*. Hong Kong: Blacksmith, 2005 (revision entitled *Hong Kong Volunteers in Battle, December 1941*, 2020).
———. "St Paul's College: A Short History". St Paul's College 120th Anniversary Souvenir Book. Hong Kong: St Paul's College, 1971.
———. The Coronation Procession in London. 1953 In the R. M. Stewart Family Collection
Stewart, Louisa. Women's Work in Fuh-kien Province. London: CMS, no date.
Stewart, Robert Warren. Letters of Robert Warren Stewart 1876–1880, CMS Archives, Central Records at Adam Matthews.
Stock, Eugene. *For Christ and Fukien: The Story of the Fukien Mission of the Church Missionary Society*, London: CMS, 1904.
———. *History of the Church Missionary Society*. 4 vols. London: Church Missionary Society, 1904–16.
Taylor, Howard, and Mrs. Howard Taylor. *Hudson Taylor and the China Inland Mission*. 2 vols. London: Morgan & Scott, 1918.
Taylor, Joseph. *A History of the West China Union University,1910–1935*. Chengdu: Canadian Mission Press, 1936.
The Dark World's Fire: Tom and Lena Edgar at War. At https://brianedgar.wordpress.com/2013/11/06wong-shiu-pun-preston/.
Tippett, Rodney W. "Australian Army Chaplains, Southwest Pacific Area, 1942–1945." MA Hons. Dissertation, Australian Defence Force Academy, University of New South Wales, 1989.
Walmsley, L. C. *West China Union University*. New York: Church Board for Christian Higher Education in China, 1974.
Wasserman, Jeffrey. *Student Protests in Twentieth Century China: The View from Shanghai*. Stanford: Stanford University Press, 1927.
Watson, Mary. *Robert and Louisa Stewart in Life and Death*. London: Marshall, 1895.
Welch, Ian. H. The Flower Mountain Murders: A Missionary Case Study Data Base Australian National University Research Publications, Canberra, 2011. At https://openresearch-repository.anu.edu.au/handle/1885/7273/.
———. "Missionaries, Murder and Diplomacy in Late 19th Century China." Paper presented to the 2nd Australian National University Missionary History Conference, 27–29 August 2006. At anglicanhistory.org/asia/china/welch_ANU2006.pdf/.

———. "'The Vegetarians': A Secret Society in Fujian Sheng province, China 1895." Paper prepared for the Asian Studies Association of Australia, University of Wollongong, New South Wales, June 2, 2006, 26–29. At https://openresearch-repository.anu.edu.au/handle/ 1885/32004?mode=full/.

———, "Women's Work for Women: Women Missionaries in 19th Century." Paper presented to the Eighth Women in Asia Conferene 2008, University of Technology, Sydney, 26–28 September 2005. anglicanhistory.org/asia/china/welch2005/.

Wellington College Yearbook 1914-20. Wellington College. At https://www.memorial.wellington.org.ac.uk/.

Wickeri, Philip. *Christian Encounters with Chinese Culture: Essays on Anglican and Episcopal History in China*. Hong Kong: Hong Kong University Press, 2015.

Wickeri, Philip, and Ruiwen Chen. *Thy Kingdom Come: A Photographic History of Anglicanism in Hong Kong, Macau, and Mainland China*. Sheng Kung Hui: Historical Studies of Anglican Christianity in China. Hong Kong: Hong Kong University, 2019.

Wittenbach, H. A. *Forward: The Motto and the Challenge of the Stewart Family*. London: CMS, 1948.

———. Tour of East Asia 1953–1954. *East Asia General Japan and China 1938–1949*.

Wolfendale, Stuart. *Imperial to International: A History of St John's Cathedral Hong Kong*. Hong Kong: Hong Kong University Press, 2013.

Worcestershire WW1 Centenary. At https:/www.ww1worcestershire.co.uk/key-dates/1916/01/chaplain-killed-at-burial-service/

Wright-Nooth, George. *Prisoner of the Turnip Heads: Horror, Hunger and Humour in Hong Kong 1941–1945*. London: Cooper, 1999.

Zarrow, Peter. *War and Revolution in China 1895–1949*. London: Routledge, 2005.

CPSIA information can be obtained
at www.ICGtesting.com
Printed in the USA
LVHW081348260123
737982LV00009B/340

9 781666 725032